Teaching as if Students Matter

D1545964

Teaching as if Students Matter

A Guide to Creating Classrooms
Based on Relationships and Engaged Learning

JAYE ZOLA AND JOHN ZOLA

Published by State University of New York Press, Albany

For information, contact State University of New York Press, Albany, NY
www.sunypress.edu

Library of Congress Cataloging-in-Publication Data

Names: Zola, Jaye, author. | Zola, John, author.
Title: Teaching as if students matter : a guide to creating classrooms
    based on relationships and engaged learning / Jaye Zola and John Zola.
Description: Albany : State University of New York Press, [2024]. | Includes
    bibliographical references and index.
Identifiers: LCCN 2023023657 | ISBN 9781438496672 (hardcover : alk. paper) |
    ISBN 9781438496696 (ebook) | ISBN 9781438496689 (pbk. : alk. paper)
Subjects: LCSH: Teacher-student relationships. | Parent-teacher
    relationships. | Teachers—Professional relationships. | Classroom
    environment. | Culturally relevant pedagogy.
Classification: LCC LB1033 .Z628 2024 | DDC 371.102/3—dc23/eng/20230721
LC record available at https://lccn.loc.gov/2023023657

10 9 8 7 6 5 4 3 2 1

To our parents, Richard and Jessie Zola,
Joan and Bernie Bloom, and David Rowland.

To our children, Natty and Peter,
and to their partners Pam and Melissa.

To our grandchildren, Nico and Felix.

We honor our past,
we work to improve the world we live in,
and we teach for the future.

Contents

Preface

Why We Wrote This Book

Music is important in the lives of adolescents. It was true for us and is probably true for you. For many years, teaching and learning have gotten little respect in the music that youth listen to. Sam Cooke in the early 1960s sang in "Wonderful World," "Don't know much about history . . ." or biology, science, and French. Paul Simon, in the 1973 song "Kodachrome," thought back on "all the crap I learned in high school" and considered it a wonder he could "even think at all." In 1983, Bruce Springsteen claimed in "No Surrender" that "we learned more from a three-minute record . . . than we ever learned in school." In 1995, Tupac said teachers "couldn't reach me." Fiona Apple in 2020 remembers being bullied in school in "Shameika." In "Fifteen" (2021), Taylor Swift wrote about starting ninth grade and needing to "stay out of everybody's way."

Each of these lyrics seems to taunt us and demean our chosen profession. They are unflattering kernels of truth about the education system. This book is our chance, as teachers, to share a different perspective on schools and learning.

Teaching is a great profession. Despite what those lyrics say, we know teaching is a wonderful, rewarding, inspiring, world-changing profession. The dismal views of teaching and learning are perhaps not far from the truth for some people, but how depressing. Teaching is a challenging and difficult job with little support, too much to do, and (compared to other professions) too little pay. On the other hand, we run into former students around town and reminisce about shared classroom experiences. We see former students' names on movie credits. They are environmental leaders and civic activists, baristas, therapists, teachers, and infographics designers. We see them as parents playing with their kids in the park. They thank us for being their teachers.

What teacher in your life has inspired you? Why?

Teaching, especially for the sort of teacher we describe in this book, is a terrific career.

- You spend your days with delightful and sometimes goofy children and adolescents, working with them based on relationship instead of power and control.

- You help young people learn and develop to become competent adults.

- You grow and get better at something you care about.

- You get to plan and teach interesting lessons about subject matter you love.

- You stay abreast of new concepts or current events and help students understand them.

- You create opportunities for students to understand a concept or create a masterful project or show compelling reasoning and thinking.

- You get a do-over every school year—an opportunity to do it better or differently and hopefully have more success. In fact, you often get that same do-over every day.

- You're actively making the world a better place!

As a teacher, you learn that if you know a pop culture reference, it's already out of date. But when you share that reference, kids look at you quizzically and with a sort of appreciation that you're trying to keep up with their lives. You get to feel old when you ask a kid what they're listening to and they name a band that *you* listened to when you were their age. You run into your students at the grocery store, and they ask, "What are you doing here?"

While there are naysayers who will question your decision to be a teacher, don't let their opinions and critiques color the reality that teaching is a profession with not only infinite struggles but also endless delights. What we do as teachers is central to building and maintaining the communities in which we want to live and thrive. Few other professions are more central to helping develop citizens who live and contribute to our democratic way of life. You model democratic skills and embody the values of equity and justice for all by teaching an anti-oppressive curriculum in your classroom. You get to nurture kids' abilities and provide them differentiated opportunities to grow and learn in ways that recognize their emotional development, gender identity, race, ethnicity, and religious tradition.

We don't want to underestimate how hard it is to be a successful teacher. It *is* hard and frustrating at times. But when you put your full self into the work, it gradually gets better. You have small victories to compensate for times when it just doesn't go as planned. We encourage novice teachers to celebrate your approximations! With practice and perseverance, it gets better and better, and soon you just know you can do this thing. It's work worth doing well.

Our local university gives out an annual award called The Best Should Teach. The premise of the award is that teaching is the foundational occupation. All other professions arise because someone teaches others how to do or be in that profession. It's a powerful charge and an important responsibility. Teaching is a great profession!

What are some reasons you're excited to be a teacher?

We offer this book to new teachers as they enter the profession, as well as to teachers already in the classroom who are interested in reflecting on their current practice. Although we spent our careers in middle and high schools, we intend this book to be a worthwhile resource for teachers of younger students and teachers in a wide range of content areas.

We wrote *Teaching as if Students Matter* as a book for teachers. It is based on our combined years of teaching in a variety of public school classrooms. This book presents our craft wisdom informed by years of taking education classes, being involved in our profession from the local to the national level, and reading and teaching using current educational theory. This is a practical guide for practitioners. Readers of *Teaching as if Students Matter* will find the research behind these teaching ideas and approaches in their foundations, educational psychology, and methods courses.

About the Authors

We are white, cisgender people. Growing up, we attended public schools in predominately white, middle-class communities. Our own school experiences were overwhelmingly positive, something we brought into our own approach to teaching. We are aware of how our upbringing and experiences influence how we view the world and schools.

We spent our careers as middle/junior high and high school social studies and humanities teachers. We do educational consulting both in the US and in other countries, working with teachers, school districts, and international schools to share the ideas we are now presenting in this book. We continue to write curriculum and volunteer in classrooms.

The schools where we began our careers were traditional in their structure and approaches to teaching. Secondary classrooms were dominated by lecture and recitation. Traditional objective tests assessed learning using true/false, fill-in-the-blank, and short answers. Teachers were in charge, and most parents deferred to the school in matters of discipline. One of the most significant changes over the length of our careers was that when we began, if there was a conflict with a student, the teacher was presumed right and the student at fault. These days, it seems almost completely reversed. Times change.

We were happy teaching in these schools because we were able to create and maintain positive relationships with students and teach well. As new, young teachers, we were motivated by a desire to make learning more engaging, interactive, and inclusive. Our goal in these traditional school settings was for all our students to have the best learning experience possible in our classrooms. We were able to create learning environments based on the ideas that we now offer in this book.

Sometimes it wasn't easy to teach what and how we believed, but we learned over time how to advocate for and champion the ideas in this book. One of our frustrations was the lack of a critical mass of teachers who shared our values and educational beliefs, but as we worked with colleagues and mentored new teachers, we extended the reach of our ideas and practices. Just about any teacher can implement the ideas in this book in their own classroom and in any type of school. A colleague once coined the phrase "rebel in the mainstream" to characterize this tension between being the teacher you want to be in your own classroom and working to change more traditional school cultures. It was hard at times to be what felt like the lone voice advocating for change, but it was important to teach in ways that felt genuine to us. We tried to be those rebels.

When teaching in traditional school settings, we enthusiastically engaged in various reform efforts at both the building and district level. Disappointingly, we found that only small things changed around the edges. We wanted something more substantive where we could implement and create a whole school based on active, engaged learning and a culture of equity and civic engagement. Midway through our careers, we had the opportunity to move out of our traditional high school to help design and open a break-the-mold public high school. New Vista High School in Boulder, Colorado, was founded with the goal of putting into practice much of what had been learned about pedagogy over the previous two decades. Enrollment was open to any student in the district through a randomized lottery, with no entrance requirements.

These were New Vista's founding principles:

• Shared respect between students and teachers

• Knowing all students well through a robust advisory system

• Active and engaged learning with persistent opportunities for meaningful voice and discussion

• Multiple opportunities for students to learn in and with the local community

• Demonstrating learning through a variety of means rather than traditional testing

• High expectations for all students and the support to meet those expectations

• Making equity for students and teachers a priority

• Respecting and honoring all students regardless of race, ethnicity, gender, sexual orientation, ability, or other "ways of being"

• A curriculum based on diversity, inclusion, equity, and justice

New Vista continues to successfully educate students in our community.

We know that most of our readers will teach or already teach in more traditional schools. But many of the once innovative or radical ideas that underpinned New Vista are finding wider acceptance in the educational community at large, particularly to counteract a culture of punitive discipline and rote learning that disproportionately affect students of color, maintain achievement gaps and high dropout rates, and increase teacher burnout. The COVID-19 pandemic only intensified the need to address many of these systemic challenges. No single reform can ameliorate these problems, but we believe that a pedagogy based in relationships, authenticity, and engaged learning is a necessary part of making education more equitable for all students in any school.

Throughout this book, we share real stories that happened to us and our colleagues to illustrate ideas and strategies that, over our decades of teaching, proved to work well in a wide range of school settings.

John's Story

I was hired in December on my last day as a student teacher. I replaced an elderly social studies teacher who just couldn't take another Midwest winter. My contract began in late January, and I had no real sense of the culture of the school where I was hired. There was no induction and no orientation to speak of. The department head handed me a textbook and a three-ring binder with an indecipherable curriculum guide. To say I was clueless would be a dramatic understatement. As a twenty-two-year-old, I'd been hired to teach eleventh-grade US history on a campus with about 2,600 eleventh- and twelfth-grade students. I was repeatedly stopped in the hallway and asked for my hall pass until the parent volunteer hall monitors began to recognize me. I depended on my colleagues for ideas about how to teach the required curriculum, while also trying to bring my fresh-out-of-college and hopefully innovative ideas into the classroom. I survived that semester and returned for three more years, until I learned about a professional development center for social studies education in Boulder. During a one-year stint there as a teacher associate, I wrote federally funded teaching materials and learned how to plan and conduct professional development workshops. It was a great year with an incredible amount of learning and no papers to grade! I spent the next year earning my master's in curriculum and instruction and working as a substitute teacher—something that maybe every teacher ought to do at some point. In six schools in two states, I taught various social studies classes from seventh to twelfth grade. Over my career I continued to write curriculum and teach teachers in a variety of settings from university classrooms to international conferences to schools in emerging democracies.

JAYE'S STORY

My first teaching job was in the junior high I had attended, and it was with colleagues who had been my teachers. I got hired the day before school started and hit the ground running. It was a traditional school, but I was able to teach how I wanted. I team taught a history/English class using a thematic approach instead of chronological history. I was also the girls' basketball coach, school store sponsor, student council sponsor, and district social studies council representative. I think the older teachers were happy to have a new teacher adding energy to the place and taking on extracurricular tasks. Being a member of the Colorado Council for the Social Studies offered me opportunities to learn from great teachers and organizations, and I eventually started to lead workshops and teacher trainings. At the district level, I was involved in efforts to improve curriculum and instruction, facilitate equity trainings, and work on national efforts to improve school climate. I enjoyed being in the classroom because these professional endeavors enriched my life and my students. In four different schools I taught social studies and humanities, and I was a librarian. I loved teaching my students, mentoring student teachers, writing curriculum, taking teachers on study tours to Japan, providing professional development at overseas conferences, and teaching online. I can't imagine any other profession that would provide such opportunities and rich connections to students, teachers, and the world.

OUR STORY

We met when we were both asked to help plan and organize a meeting of the Rocky Mountain Regional Social Studies Conference in Denver. It turned out that we shared educational and personal values. We immediately started dating and sharing teaching ideas. Not long after, we were married. The week of our wedding, John was hired at a middle school in a neighboring school district. We taught at different schools for two years until our first child was born. Jaye's school allowed us to do a job-sharing arrangement where each of us taught for a half day and parented for the other half. The pay wasn't great, but we were able to co-parent and maintain our careers as teachers. Luckily, we had opportunities to write curriculum and teaching activities for small publishing houses and social studies curriculum development centers. This provided extra income and helped us become better teachers.

We had an opportunity to transfer from the junior high school to a high school and continue job sharing, which gave us the chance to teach many of our students for the six years they were in secondary education. Talk about having long-term relationships with your students! We came to know them well. Several years later, we both helped create and teach at New Vista. There, we had the opportunity to implement our ideas about engaged and authentic learning and our values related to diversity, equity, and inclusion. Since retirement, we've continued to write curriculum, conduct professional development workshops, coach colleagues, and work in local and international schools.

Who Should Read This Book?

We, and probably most teachers, entered the field because we wanted to do something good for and with young people. Some of us became teachers to share a passion for our content area. Some might have known the value of working and interacting with young people or thought teaching could have a positive impact on our collective futures. Whatever our own reasons, we probably didn't become teachers to bore students, shout ineffectively at persistent misbehavior, or grumble about the latest imposition on our time during a required professional development day.

Teaching is one of those professions where we bring a great deal of who we are into the workplace. Our approach requires a willingness to be open to self-critique and new insights. Perhaps most important, it requires an openness to sharing authority in the classroom and welcoming all students to be collaborators in their own learning. The ideas in this book are most suitable for individuals who find excitement in working with others to achieve shared success.

We know from our years of working with new and early-career teachers that what we offer in this book is lacking in most professional development training, which includes little time or attention paid to developing and sustaining the relationships that are central to working with young people and colleagues. Of course, no one book or single approach to teaching can magically smooth the transition into the teaching profession or solve the problems facing public education. But there *is* a way to do better for students and for ourselves and to avoid the experiences and attitudes reflected in those song lyrics that open this preface.

Here are some of the readers we envision benefiting from this book:

- **Pre-service teacher candidates.** This book explains how we believe teachers can create relationships with students and set up their classrooms and instruction to do so successfully. Pre-service teachers can explore the ideas in this book with other practitioners at school sites and with professors in classes on methods and foundations of education.

- **New teachers.** What we have to say challenges some of the more traditional advice given to novice teachers. New, enthusiastic teachers who want to personalize their teaching and provide engaged instruction will find specific suggestions and tools to help accomplish these goals and supplement their work with induction coaches and mentors.

- **Classroom teachers of all content areas and grade levels.** Teaching is an ever-revitalizing profession, and every teacher can find new or different ways to think about their pedagogy and their relationships with students. Our experience and expertise lie in the secondary grades, but the core ideas and principles we advocate are also appropriate and adaptable for elementary classrooms.

Good teaching transcends grade level and content. We taught social studies and the humanities, so many of our stories and ideas come from those experiences, but we know that teachers of science, math, physical education, art, and other subjects can base their classrooms and instruction on the key approaches we explore in this book. At the same time, we recognize and value the pedagogical content knowledge that allows for the special experiences and ways of learning that distinguish the sciences from the arts, math from the humanities.

We offer this book to teachers who want to approach each day with a sense of optimism and excitement when engaging with their students. Our profession comes with myriad distractions and downers, but we believe that each day and each student should be greeted with a positive and engaging affect. What a bummer to start the day with someone who thinks the day will be a bummer! Teaching well done is a noble profession, but it is hard and often messy work. Teachers make mistakes and face challenges every day. Students resist our best efforts and lessons fail. And yet, teachers return every day to try again.

We hope you find the ideas, advice, and stories helpful as you enter this terrific profession and grow within it.

How This Book Is Organized

In the introduction we present the big ideas that persist throughout the book: relationships, authenticity, the democratic purposes of schools, and cultural responsiveness. Chapter 1 looks in depth at relationships, which are at the very heart of what we think teaching and learning is all about. Chapter 2 focuses on classroom management. No matter how innovative your pedagogy or creative your lessons, you need solid management systems in place so all students can feel safe and available for learning. As you'll see, there is a tight connection between relationships and the management of behavior in the classroom.

Chapters 3 delves into planning for authentic and engaging instruction, with an emphasis on the nuts and bolts and the practicalities of teaching through relationship. Chapter 4 emphasizes the importance of student voice and discussion as ways of making meaning and fostering the democratic purposes of schools, as well as how to teach controversial issues. In chapter 5, we address how assessment and feedback can support student success. We also talk about grading and homework. Chapter 6 discusses how to develop and maintain good relationships with colleagues and how to work with parents and families. We explore ways to stay engaged in teaching without burning out and about how being healthy is central to your own well-being and effectiveness in the classroom.

As you read and interact with the ideas in this book, we hope you are prompted to recall vignettes from your own schooling or your current practice. Take time to reflect on the questions we pose. This book can motivate you to be a great teacher and support you as you grow toward being the teacher you want to be.

In this book we've combined our philosophy of education based on sound pedagogy with the practical demands of everyday teaching. We believe how we teach is interwoven with how we show up in schools and classrooms. This includes our senses of self, humor, integrity, and growth as culturally responsive educators. The more we are our authentic selves with students, the more they can allow and reveal themselves to us. But that's not enough. Teaching is a highly developed craft that demands a wide range of skills and dispositions. This book is our attempt to meld these two important dimensions so you can teach all students well.

You can find additional resources to support the ideas and activities in this book at www.teachingasifstudentsmatter.com.

Introduction

The Core Ideas of This Book

The core ideas that weave their way through this book are *relationships*, *authenticity*, *cultural responsiveness*, and the *democratic purposes of schools*. When we teach from relationship, offer authentic learning experiences, and engage in culturally responsive practices, we embody the democratic purposes of schooling. It is in our classrooms that students practice the skills and dispositions associated with meaningful participation in our democratic society.

> What are some of the core ideas you hold about teaching and learning? How are they similar or different from these four core ideas?

Relationships

The relationships we can create with students are at the heart of being an effective teacher. Nearly every classroom problem—not doing homework, discipline, emotional trauma, motivation—can be prevented, resolved, or improved through a positive relationship between student and teacher. This means teaching is first and foremost a human enterprise, an endeavor that involves at least two human beings of different status and age and perhaps race, culture, sexual orientation, or religion meeting in the shared spaces of the classroom and school. When we acknowledge and understand this, teaching takes on an entirely different look and feel. Good relationships between teachers and students help make the school

1

a safe learning environment where every student can bring their whole self to the classroom. Kids can be motivated and challenged academically when they are treated with respect and are known and valued.

When relationships are central, students are less fearful of ridicule or being unnoticed and can more confidently participate in discussions, contribute their ideas, make mistakes, invest in classroom activities, and achieve their potential. This can only happen when the teacher cultivates a classroom climate where encouragement, equity, authenticity, and real-life engagement are promoted and supported through relationship. A teacher's classroom management, instructional choices, and professional growth should all be motivated by a commitment to creating positive relationships with students.

Relationships are at the heart of making classrooms safe for all students to learn and grow socially and emotionally. Anxiety, depression, teen suicide, drug abuse, school shootings, and other mental health and behavioral issues are on the rise. The legacies of racism, oppression, and inequity have made classrooms unsafe for non-majority children. Schools and classrooms are part of the problem because they are a microcosm of the larger society, but they are also places where we can address these problems as we create safety and engagement. Relationships are the foundation for creating an environment where students and teachers thrive so they can participate in the rigors of discussion and in-depth, engaging activities. Classrooms built on relationships invite students to bring their most authentic selves to the classroom.

Authenticity

We use the term *authenticity* in two ways. First, teachers must be willing to engage students when teaching and building relationships with their most authentic self. This means that teachers must be genuine when interacting with students and colleagues. Young people are pretty crafty BS detectors. It's hard enough to create and nurture relationships when being authentic; it's even harder when putting on a fake persona or valuing power more than the work of developing relationships. Teacher-student relationships built on authenticity can weather tough times. Students are more motivated to meet high expectations when they know the caring is real. Trust, joy, and humor are also necessary for building authentic relationships. Together, they can create an environment of positive human interaction that we believe is at the heart of healthy, engaged, and challenging classrooms.

Authenticity also applies to instructional activities, which should be more connected to real life than the worksheets and graphic organizers that are so frequently found in classrooms. The more authentic or real the activity, the more likely students will be to buy in and engage in challenging and powerful learning. Solving real-world scientific or mathematical problems, discussing actual policy dilemmas facing the community, drawing examples from a student's life, and writing for real audiences are ways to bring authenticity to your instruction and make learning relevant to students.

Cultural Responsiveness

As teachers and as members of a democratic society, we recognize that oppression by the dominant culture exists in the form of racism, heterosexism, classism, anti-LGBTQIA+, xenophobia, and other forms of intolerance that result in inequities for nondominant cultures and people. All students and families in our communities, regardless of their identities, should be equally valued members of the school community. A commitment to equity requires persistent effort to root out structural racism, sexism, homophobia, religious intolerance, and other isms. Too many young people have been marginalized and disrespected in schools. It takes conscious and specific effort to redress past injustices and to invite every student into the learning process.

If all students are to learn in our classrooms, we must honor and give validity to their experiences, voices, and identities. One way to do this is to use and respect the ways they self-identify. We want to note our use of pronouns in this book. We use *they*, *them*, or *their* as singular pronouns, not just *he*, *she*, *him*, or *her*. We think this is more inclusive and allows space for individuals to identify themselves in ways of their own choosing.

The Democratic Purposes of Schools

Our public education system exists, most importantly, to help students learn, practice, and nurture the values of our democratic society. It is in our public education system that students of all ages come to appreciate and promote core democratic values:

- Equity

- Anti-racism

- Treating others with respect

- Listening

- Agreeing to disagree responsibly

- Open-mindedness

- Forming opinions based on facts

- Taking turns

- Engaging in civic activities

- Justice for all

We want students in our classrooms to learn to be civil in society, to recognize that democracy is an evolving political system, and to see themselves as effective actors in making our society more just. These ideals were articulated at the founding of the nation, and despite a rise in polarization, the power of social media, and laws limiting what teachers can teach, these same ideals remain central to why we compel all young people to attend school. Private schools and charter schools are not exempt from this duty; their students must also learn to share the classroom space and the larger society with others who are different from themselves.

Schools and classrooms should be places where students become familiar with the concepts and values associated with social justice. Learning about the causes of inequality and working to end it are important aspects of being a citizen in a democracy. Human rights and equity should be modeled and taught in schools. In a democracy, we have the responsibility to make the world a more just place. Indeed, schools are among the few places in society where young people learn about the balance and tension between rights and responsibilities in a democracy.

Not everyone in this democracy believes that schools are places for promoting justice or equity. Efforts have been made, for example, to limit teaching about systemic racism. State legislatures have passed laws on what topics teachers can or cannot address in classrooms and at what ages. Bills have been passed that limit what books can be assigned or found in the school library. As teachers, we can use our rights as citizens to protest these laws and help educate our communities about the importance of open inquiry, the risks that censorship has to a free and open democratic society, and how to support the fight for social justice. But we are also public employees who are subject to these sorts of legislation. Each of us makes our individual choices when facing these challenges. This book provides guidance on how to negotiate these pressures while supporting the democratic purposes of schools.

Within a society that is increasingly self-segregating into like-minded communities of socioeconomic and political affiliations, schools and classrooms should be safe places to encounter differences of opinion and background. These are critical experiences for future civic participation and engagement. Many of the skills and types of student engagement we advocate in this book support our democratic core values and develop the role of citizen.

Instilling these values is not the sole responsibility of social studies classes. Collaborative work in math and science classrooms supports the values of democracy. Fair play in physical education classes models how citizens should interact in a democracy. Puzzling out ethical dilemmas in the sciences, from cloning to climate change, is a task for all citizens. Reading stories to elementary school children about different groups starts modeling inclusion. Students should come to see the centrality of liberty in a democracy as they learn the stories and struggles of marginalized peoples in the literature they read and in the people they meet.

There are powerful connections between the interpersonal relationships we advocate for our classrooms and the civic relationships that undergird a functioning democracy. Teachers and students forge bonds of mutual respect and appreciation that cross boundaries of power and age to do meaningful work in the classroom. A democracy depends on equally healthy and respectful relationships among citizens to serve the civic good and promote social justice. When the bonds of relationship among citizens are frayed or stretched, we see polarization and dysfunction in society. The same is true in our classrooms. Thus, the democratic purpose of schools is intimately and powerfully connected to the development of meaningful and productive relationships in our classrooms.

Classrooms with healthy relationships between teachers and students and where learning tasks are more authentic are, by their very nature, more democratic. These classrooms are mini laboratories for participating in civil society. Classrooms like this allow for greater student voice and choice in learning opportunities and empower students to take on real-life tasks. As they do these things, students are practicing the tasks and skills of citizens. In these classrooms, inclusion and equity are celebrated and honored by modeling and practicing how to live and learn among diverse members of the larger community.

Think back to your own school experiences. What are your memories of relationships, authenticity, cultural responsiveness, and the promotion of democratic values? If you can't think of any, why might that be?

Chapter 1

It All Begins with Relationships

Relationships are at the center of our approach to teaching. This means getting to know your students from the first day and caring about them as unique individuals. It means showing authentic concern for them: who they are, their interests, what they do outside of the classroom, and their lives as they overlap and intersect with yours. Students who have strong relationships with their teachers feel seen, known, and understood. This connection allows them to care more about themselves, their classmates, and their schoolwork. The connections between student and teacher don't require affection, but caring is essential. Your relationships with students' families and your colleagues are equally important. The goal is to create whatever connections are possible. It's not effortless or easy, but it is possible and important.

What you'll find in this chapter:

- Why relationships are important to being an effective teacher

- How relationships between teachers and students change from kindergarten through twelfth grade (K–12)

- Ways to overcome the obstacles in creating positive relationships

- Why cultural responsiveness is crucial to building relationships with students

- How positive interactions with students in the hallways and other public spaces at school help build relationships

- How to create and maintain clear boundaries with students, even as you show your care and concern

- How your experiences as a student influence your choices and actions as a teacher

Taking an interest in every student creates connections that are the foundation of classrooms where there is a sense of belonging and where students feel safe and motivated to learn. Students who have strong relationships with their teachers commit to doing more challenging assignments. They are more willing to seriously consider teacher feedback on assignments and revise them to meet expectations. A teacher who knows a student well can provide encouragement and motivation, as well as more personalized learning opportunities. These supports that come from relationships help bridge the achievement gap.

Unfortunately, in today's world many students come to our classrooms having experienced trauma. These emotional experiences are not left at the schoolhouse doors. It is difficult for a student to learn if they have a parent with cancer or a mental illness, if they live in a shelter or are homeless, if there is domestic abuse, if there is gun violence, or if their parents might be deported. If a student has been harmed by discrimination in school, their toxic experience is brought into the classroom. Your classroom may be the one safe and caring space for a child. We wouldn't expect someone to do a class project with a broken bone sticking out of their arm. Likewise, we need to address the social and emotional issues that can get in the way of learning. This is why we stress building relationships as a core theme of this book.

We know that adolescence and the teen years are emotionally challenging for many students in our schools. The power of social media seems to continue unchecked and with a variety of harmful effects on teen well-being. Teenagers report increasing levels of sadness, thoughts of suicide, and experiences of violence. This is especially true for LGBTQIA+ students and students questioning their gender identity. A problem of this magnitude requires interventions at many points of society, but one crucial form of support can be the relationships teachers build with their students. Schools can make a profound difference by increasing the sense among all students that they are cared for, supported, and belong. Teachers can be allies and trusted adults for students. Being known, heard, and valued is so important to teens who are facing the pressures of an increasingly complicated society.

Over the course of our careers, educational movements have emerged that stress the importance of students' healthy emotional and social development so they can be fully present to learn. Efforts to make this central in the teaching profession have had many names—*affective education*, *character development*, and *conflict resolution*, to name just a few. A recent iteration is *social and emotional learning* (SEL). Teachers who value relationships pay attention to their students' social and emotional well being. It is essential if students are to engage fully in their learning.

Teachers who know their students have more tools to help them succeed academically, socially, and emotionally. Skilled educators know that social and emotional learning must be incorporated into daily instruction and the classroom climate. Students need opportunities to learn skills and attitudes associated with self-awareness, self-management, social awareness, relationship building, and responsible decision making. When these skills are recognized, nurtured, practiced, and honored, the teacher-student relationship becomes instrumental to student success.

The importance of building and nurturing relationships in classrooms became even more apparent during the COVID-19 pandemic. The cancellation of in-person learning challenged the building of relationships because teachers could not interact with their students in the classroom. They had to learn how to develop relationships online, finding brief moments to connect and to get to know their students. Video conferencing, threaded conversations, texting, or other forms of media were of limited value. There is nothing like teaching in person to get to know your students well.

Another emotional stress for both students and teachers comes from the epidemic of school shootings. Relationships are one of the ways to be available for our students as they face the fears they may bring into the classroom. We are able to support our kids when practicing active shooter drills and talk about the fears that arise each time there is a shooting somewhere.

Positive relationships with students can also diminish discord in the classroom. Conflicts that often impede learning can be mitigated and addressed through conversation and shared problem solving instead of power and control. We use the phrase *power and control* to characterize the more traditional interactions between teachers and students that are based in the institutional authority of the teacher over the student. The teacher does have responsibility for student learning and appropriate behavior, but relationships based on shared power create a more successful teaching and learning environment.

A bright and persistently off-task student kept ignoring prompts to focus and get down to work. I invited her aside and asked what was going on. She said she was trying to see if she could get me angry. My response was, "So, how's that working for you so far?" I asked a question to make her think. No escalation and no shouting were needed. Instead, we started to make a plan together with rewards and consequences for how the next part of the day would unfold. That day went better. She had been cared for and valued, regardless of how well she performed in the class and despite her explicit goal of being disruptive. Her off-task behaviors generally persisted, but we continued to rely on relationship, and by the end of the year her demeanor had improved markedly, and she was more engaged in school.

Getting to Know Your Students

Relationships begin simply, on the first day, with a greeting as kids enter the classroom. They develop further when the teacher asks how a student's day is going or how they're doing. You might ask about an interest or what they're listening to on their headphones. You might chat about sports, school activities, fingernail polish, or how they get to school every day. Notice them and talk about what you see them doing. Use their name. If a student resists these efforts, don't push too hard, too quickly. Take small steps and use patience and perseverance. This is important whether you are interacting with the self-motivated, high-self-esteem student or the one hiding in the back of the class.

One early August day, a young woman walked up to us while we were playing with our five-year-old son in our front yard. She introduced herself as Denise and said she would be our son's kindergarten teacher in the new school year. As we chatted, our son was clearly curious about who she was. After a moment, Denise asked if she could speak with him separately. Off they went, and we stood back, sort of marveling at the interaction. Denise kneeled down so she was at his level and said hello. She asked questions, and he shyly replied. Soon they came back to us. He was holding a cardboard circle on a piece of yarn. He proudly explained that this would be his name tag for the first day, and he was to color it however he wanted. The smile on his face was priceless. We, two seasoned educators about to become public school parents, couldn't have been happier! When we dropped him off on the first day of school, he walked right in the door and never looked back.

This was the beginning of the type of relationship we want students to have with their teachers throughout their K–12 education. Denise took the time to care about our son as an individual and ask about his interests. She assigned him an authentic task that had relevance to a new kindergarten student and welcomed him to her classroom. Every student you teach is somebody's kid whose family wants the best for them. That is what we felt when Denise welcomed our son to kindergarten. Unfortunately, not all teachers can visit their students, but this illustrates one way to begin to make connections with students. A variety of activities and get-to-know-you games in the classroom can help teachers begin forming relationships with their students. Taking the time to do this helps you learn about your kids so you can better connect learning to their lives.

The K–12 Erosion of Relationships

Creating and nurturing relationships is hard work. Along with dealing with student behavior and teaching, we have competing demands and expectations of our time, including committee work, collegial relationships, teacher administrative duties, and parent requests. Teachers also have to run active shooter drills and respond to social and political issues and even natural hazards that inevitably intrude on the classroom. Together, these can create serious challenges to building and maintaining relationships, but we know that relationships are essential for student learning. We can't let other responsibilities distract us from our real job of teaching human beings.

Our own biases, stereotypes, and prior school experiences can also get in the way of building relationships. It takes work to consciously attend to every student who comes into our classroom. It can be uncomfortable chatting with a wide variety of students in the hallways or in the cafeteria who might be quite different from us or who don't know us. Our job is to be role models who accept, are interested in, and engage equally with every type of students we encounter. Students see this and take cues from our behaviors. This is modeling for social and emotional learning, as well as equity. If we want to teach from relationship, we must be the ones who work to form those relationships.

Elementary, middle, and high school each present unique challenges to developing relationships with students. They include issues of class size, content demands, cultural differences, child and adolescent development, and testing of behavior. These affect how we develop rapport with our students and fellow staff. As kids move through the grades, relationship building is challenging in other ways. Teachers seem to use more power and control when interacting with older students, and the demands and requirements of postsecondary education can reduce opportunities for student choice. These factors and time pressures make relationships harder to form. Relationships can easily become more transactional than nurturing with older students.

Elementary students often have significant responsibilities in their classroom and for their learning. They clean up the room, help set up learning stations, have choices for reading, and can often move freely around the classroom. They sit at tables where they work with their classmates, not rows of desks. They frequently work in small groups or teams of varying sizes. Part of why this works is that most elementary teachers know their students well enough to structure learning situations that are more personalized. Even in kindergarten, students are given appropriate degrees of choice and independence in their learning.

From kindergarten through the earliest years of school, many elementary teachers value and attend to relationships. They make time throughout the school day for the spontaneous interactions that help build their relationships with students, and they can get to know students and their families well. Even in an environment of increased testing and pressure to meet external standards, much of the learning can still be based on exploration.

For most students, middle school is an increasingly impersonal experience as they adapt to schedules with multiple classes and teachers. With teachers having responsibility for up to 175 students over the course of the day, lessons often include fewer opportunities for student choice. Creating relationships and getting to know kids individually is harder, but it can be done. Many middle school teachers really do like and value these often sweet and silly young adolescents and enjoy interacting with them. Still, in middle schools most students sit at desks and instruction becomes more dependent on textbooks. They often no longer move about as freely in the classroom as they did in elementary school.

The move to high school makes establishing and nurturing relationships with students even more challenging, with larger class sizes, bigger buildings, and different rates of adolescent development. Even more than in middle school, there is little time for play or small-group work. Classrooms are characterized by rows of desks and instruction that depends on textbooks and prescribed curriculum. Students have limited choice in what they learn, with the teacher usually in front of the classroom in charge of instruction.

We know that one of the primary jobs of high school students is to individuate and create their own identity apart from their families. It is very important for them to have non-family adults with whom to connect, which is why developing positive relationships with teachers is so vital. Most students are quite happy interacting with their teachers when they feel respected, are given positive attention, and are engaged in their learning.

Table 1.1. Positive and negative factors affecting teacher-student relationships in traditional settings

Elementary school	Middle school/ junior high	High school
+ Smaller buildings + Same teacher/ students all day + Students developmentally connect to adults + Teacher is child focused + Students have responsibilities and choices + Activity and movement during the day − Online learning makes learning through play and social interaction difficult − Testing begins in intermediate grades − Teacher must get students ready for middle school	+ Students are interested in relationships with teachers + A nice mix of naïve and developing maturity + Mix of content-focused and student-focused teachers − Online learning is more difficult for middle schoolers who have less executive function and cannot pay attention for long periods of time − Larger building − More students and larger class loads − Changing classes makes it harder to be known − Shorter periods − Less choice and responsibility − Desks and textbooks − Testing − Teacher must get students ready for high school	+ Maturity helps students behave in more adult ways + Students often have interesting and sophisticated views on the world around them + Students want to be treated more like adults than children + Clubs and extracurricular activities provide meaningful opportunities for teacher-student relationships + Online learning can individualize learning for self-motivated students − Even larger building − More students − Greater class loads − Semester-based classes − Teachers are more content focused − Students are less willing to engage with adults − Students individuating − Desks, textbooks − Testing − Teachers must get students ready for postsecondary options − Fewer choices and less responsibility

> What actions for developing positive relationships in the classroom do you want to focus on as teacher?

Where to Start

It's almost too obvious to state but learning student names and correctly pronouncing them from the very first encounter is the first step in building relationships—between the teacher and students and among students. We worked hard on the first day of school to learn and remember names. It took a bit of vulnerability on our part to call on students and get it wrong or ask for help before calling on them. It's worth the awkwardness because names are at the core of every person's identity and the key to being recognized and noticed.

Knowing Names to Build Relationships

Learn each student's name and how to pronounce it in the way the student pronounces it. Don't automatically accept an anglicized pronunciation. Using the real pronunciation is important and shows respect.

When you take roll, ask students about themselves or their names so you can attach something memorable to who they are. When you learn about students, it's easier to remember their names.

Be willing to be vulnerable by calling students by name in class and in the hallways and asking for help if you forget or goof up on their name.

Use a seating chart at the beginning of the year if it helps you to learn names. You don't have to keep it after you know everyone in your class.

Play name games at the beginning of the year so all students know each other's names. Most secondary students cannot name every student in their classes at the end of the semester or school year. This is important for building a classroom community.

Use name tents, especially when you know you're going to have a class discussion. This helps students associate ideas with names and faces. It helps you learn names, too. Put the student's name on both sides of the name tent so all students can see it!

Avoid roll call after a couple of days–nothing says you don't care more than a rote listing of names.

Leave notes for substitute teachers on pronunciation and challenges in names. The substitute inaccurately reading names can be horrifying for some students.

Knowing your students' names can improve classroom management and instruction. You're modeling how to treat others in the classroom, which makes for a safer environment for participating and learning. You're valuing students as individuals, not just the work they do. For some, it might be the only time during the day that they are recognized, appreciated, or noticed in a welcoming or positive way. Kids like that.

> Driving to work each day, I do a mental check-in on my students. I visually go through a class and spend a second thinking about each kid. "Oh, that's right! I told José I would ask Mr. Johnson if he could do a project that fits both our classes." "Oh no, I haven't really touched base with Noni in a couple of days." Sometimes I do this when I'm scanning my attendance roster—I skim over the names to think about how everyone is doing. When I grade papers, I mentally check in with what I have noticed about each kid over the last few days. Leaving positive notes on homework is a great way to connect. Sometimes I write, "That was a great comment you made in discussion on Tuesday." Or I might write, "Check in with me after class and let me know how things are with you." These are little ways I stay in touch.

How Power Structures Affect Student Engagement

Many students have experienced schools as welcoming places with plenty of positive interactions with fellow students, teachers, and other adults. They find meaning in learning, sports, or extracurriculars. They move through school facing little more than the usual, though certainly not trivial, challenges associated with growing up. Everything we encourage in this book should help make their experiences better and richer. Other students, however, especially as they grow older, may become increasingly hardened in their interactions with teachers. Repeated failures, being belittled or ignored, feeling bored and not challenged with authentic learning—it's no surprise that some students feel disrespected and disengaged at school. Many non-majority students have not experienced equity or justice in their lives. Students of color have to deal with both overt and more subtle forms of systemic racism and cultural insensitivity. These students have known multiple oppressions because of the dominant narrative of white culture and economic exploitation. Gender bias and homophobia affect many young people at school. Girls and young women may have been talked over or not listened to.

You have power in the classroom because you are the teacher, you are the adult, you have a college degree, and you have the authority granted to you by the school and the school culture. This authority is built on an implicit power structure that assumes students are white, middle/upper class, and native born. As a result, the curriculum, instruction, and school norms default to white culture. If you have trouble with this notion, think about how you have felt in a situation where you were the minority—perhaps in a different country or a part of town with a different ethnic group or visiting a family with a different religious tradition. You don't know the norms or the cultural rules and it can be uncomfortable. White teachers need to acknowledge, examine, and challenge this power structure.

Students of color and English language learners are often aware of the dominance of white culture but may not know its rules, language, and norms. Teachers must recognize how these power structures affect the engagement of these students and publicly address it. This lets students know that they do not have some internal deficit as learners or as human beings. Hear what students have to say on this topic. To help them overcome this built-in disadvantage and to be fair, you need to explicitly teach the expectations and skills required to succeed in your school. Some examples of this are notions of being on time, how different age groups interact, and the why and how of classroom rules and styles of conversation.

This will be much easier to accomplish if you have created an environment with an emphasis on acceptance, community, and relationships. These efforts model and explicitly teach classroom norms and behaviors, and they empower all your students to use their voice, wrestle with ambiguity, and do authentic tasks. In this way, you will create a more successful learning community. You will have created a more equitable playing field where all can succeed.

Expanding How to View Our World

White culture shapes the values and norms of our institutions, our media, and the way we see ourselves and each other. This can be harmful because these cultural expectations are often used without being named, are the basis of comparisons, or may not be a nondominant culture's values. Dominant culture values operate in insidious ways and affect us all, whether we admit it or not. White cultural values, white ways of thinking, behaving, deciding, and knowing may ignore and disempower other ways of being. It isn't easy to examine something that exists unconsciously. When we name and point out the general white cultural values, we become aware of how to make classrooms more inclusive of different ways of being.

Just a couple examples might point out the differences.

Most schooling tends to value:	Being inclusive of other values would include valuing:
Competition and transactional relationships	Collaboration and transformational relationships
Paternalism	Partnership
Power hoarding	Power sharing
Individualism	Community, caring, and collectivism
Standard American English only	Honoring other languages as represented in different cultures, power structures, lived experience, and geography
Verbal/linguistic and logical/mathematical intelligences	Multiple modes of being–musical, visual/spatial, kinesthetic, interpersonal, and intrapersonal intelligences

As teachers we can examine how white culture is set up in our schools and how it privileges white learners as well as white teachers. To counter white privilege, we need to create classrooms where processes, structures, and practices value relationships and relationship building. How one teaches must recognize the different ways inclusion looks in the classroom. Teachers must use relationship building to know a student and to learn and respect the diversity of ways they develop, learn, and express knowledge. Relationships can provide a space for students to develop their full authentic selves.

Challenging a power structure and being open to other ways of being is a threat to some people. How do you feel about privilege and its impact on teaching?

Detoxing the School Experience

You will likely encounter students of all backgrounds who resent the power relationships that have characterized so many of their previous school and classroom interactions. They may have experienced bias and prejudice from teachers and been silenced. Some nontraditional students may choose not to play the game of school anymore and drop out or anesthetize themselves with drugs and alcohol. Some whose social and emotional needs are not addressed may cause havoc to get attention. When their past relationships with school have clearly been toxic, we call the hard work of building connections with these students "detoxing their school experience." It takes time and patience to help them rebuild a relationship with school and with teachers. This work is based on building mutual trust by working with the student's experiences, identity, and beliefs to slowly replace their learned skepticism.

The students who come to our classrooms with cynical or negative notions of what school is supposed to be about expect an unequal power dynamic between teacher and students. These students play a game where they persistently challenge the power that teachers are supposed to have over them in the classroom. They do this to gain their own power or to draw attention to themselves or because they just don't know any other way to act. The teacher has to somehow manage these students, and it's especially difficult because the behaviors can be based on the implicit white power structure or destructive interactions in prior school experiences or dysfunctional family dynamics. These students come to the teacher-student relationship with skepticism, doubt, hostility, a lack of trust, and defensiveness.

By just the third day of the new school year, I knew this was going to be a really tough kid to build a relationship with, let alone engage in classroom activities. Chaos seemed to follow Travis the moment he walked into the classroom. When the bell rang and it was time to get started, there was always a challenge: Why are we doing this? I don't have the handout. And on and on. I'm patient, I thought to myself. I can last longer being patient than he can last being a total and disruptive pain. I soon came to question this assumption as he disrupted small groups, his language crossed agreed-upon barriers, and other students seemed swept into his chaotic orbit. He would act out, then I'd say we need to chat outside, and I would tell the class to continue with their work. Because my expectations were clear and they knew what to do, the class was pretty good at carrying on in moments like this. My challenge was to find some way to make a connection with Travis. I was committed at all costs to not shouting at or threatening him. That is what he was used to, what he expected, and what he was setting me up to do. Instead, I'd ask what might make the class more engaging for him. I'd remind him about class agreements and remind him that we won't have a problem if he follows what we all agreed on at the beginning of the year. Or I'd explain that we don't talk that way in this classroom and ask if he could say what he'd said more appropriately.

I don't know exactly when, but slowly, slowly we started to connect. His entry into the classroom got less obnoxious as I'd ask how his day went or about his favorite band. I said hello to him in the hallway. I tried to chat with him and his friends in the smoking area during class breaks. I know the looks I got from Travis were just above the level of begrudging tolerance. There were also times when he and I went to have conversations with the principal, which may have set the process back a bit. But there were moments when he engaged in the work we were doing in the classroom. And then, out to the hallway for another conversation about why he was doing something clearly inappropriate.

We weathered the entire term together and even had a couple of lighter moments. I never did pull the power card on him, and a couple of years later I saw him out in the community. I knew he'd eventually dropped out of school, but he remembered his time with me as one of the few times in his school career when a teacher cared about and listened to him. He valued that, in retrospect. I guess I did no harm . . . and maybe a bit of good.

Because the teacher comes to the relationship with a disproportionate amount of power, and in the case of a white teacher embodies dominant cultural power, we must be the ones to create the space and allow the time it takes for positive relationships to develop. Creating a relationship involves a tremendous amount of patience and persistence that must begin with the teacher.

As you can see from the story about Travis, creating a relationship with a student who is challenging can involve many kinds of interactions to keep the focus on building the relationship. While there is no one magic solution, there are lots of ways to take positive steps.

- Be patient. Don't get mad—take some deep breaths and don't take their behavior personally. View disciplinary issues from a distance to develop a perspective on the situation.

- Remember that this is a young person whose behavior is telling you something, even if the way they are communicating it is inappropriate.

- Make sure you're not punishing a student who may not know the rules, language, and culture of the school's power structure.

- Set expectations and hold students to them in a firm and consistent yet kind way.

- Look for options in the curriculum and choices around assignments that might give the student some control over their learning.

- Find interests that allow you to develop a relationship that isn't focused only on the discipline issues.

- Use humor and be careful to never resort to humiliation, sarcasm, or name calling.

- Get information and help from a counselor, administrator, or colleague.

We'll have a lot more to say throughout the book about how solid relationships with students can improve classroom management and instruction.

> What was your relationship to school and schooling as you grew up? Can you think of experiences or evidence of the various power dynamics at play, including those related to white, majority assumptions underlying how schools do business?

Other Power Dynamics in the Classroom

A key to building relationships with students is not confronting student behavior with power but instead figuring out what is really going on for the student. Behavior issues need to be understood, addressed, and managed by careful listening and observing, as well as practicing patience. It means taking deep breaths and waiting for your own anger or frustration to pass or recede.

> On the first day of school in an eleventh-grade class, everyone in the room seems to be on their best behavior. After I take roll, we gather in a circle in chairs to start a get-to-know-you activity. The students mostly don't know each other, and I don't know most of them either. We're a few minutes into the activity when I hear a ball bouncing. Looking around, I see a boy bouncing a small ball between his legs as students are sharing information about themselves. My initial reaction is, "You have to be kidding me! Really?" I want to tell him to stop. It's rude—we are listening to others. His head is down, his shoulders are hunched, and he is just focused on that ball. I begin thinking the kid is saying to me and the class, "Look at me. I'm the bad kid. Go ahead give me attention and tell me to put the ball away. I'm testing you."
>
> I believe my job is to try to catch kids being good and avoid challenging inappropriate behaviors, if possible. But what about now? The bouncing doesn't actually bother me, but I feel I should do something as the teacher. Now I'm fascinated to see how this will play out, and at the same time I'm anxious that I might lose control of the class and

the activity. But I don't say anything and carry on with the activity. As he keeps bouncing the ball, the other students start getting annoyed. Will they say something? I wait and hold my tongue. Suddenly the ball gets away from him and bounces toward me. My heart is racing, but I realize what to do. I pick up the ball, look at it, and then bounce it back to him. As I do, I give him a smile and a nod that implies, "Enough." There seems to be almost a gasp from the other students. He catches his ball, puts it in his pocket, and we continue the activity.

It would have been natural to just immediately tell him to put the ball away, but waiting to do something proved helpful. I never said anything to him about the ball bouncing, then or later. He and I developed a great relationship over the semester. I had avoided a power struggle, in part by being patient. I acknowledged his negative behavior without giving him undue attention. The class also saw a different interaction between teacher and student based on acceptance, patience, and relationship building.

Building relationships means believing that students are good humans and are worthy of respect and trust. This is also where humor plays a large role. By laughing off some misbehavior or giving kids an expression that says, "This is enough goofiness," you can build relationships with some of your most challenging students. This isn't laughing at the student or with the other students. It's appreciating a young person's growing selfhood and not treating it like an affront to you. It's a bigger-picture laugh (and groan) at human foibles.

Building relationships involves accumulating lots and lots of small victories. With each positive experience of seeing the teacher act with patience and humor instead of power and control, more and more students will buy into the relationship model. At some point, you reach a critical mass where most students will be interacting with you and each other based on relationship and connection instead of power and confrontation. The going then gets easier, and the classroom climate takes on new and positive dimensions.

There might be administration support for teachers with classroom problems and they can support us when conflicts arise with students. The truth, however—as just about any novice teacher will tell you—is that whatever power we may think we have can feel very tenuous. Facing a roomful of students is daunting, and a common default is to try and promote an "I'm in charge" persona based on power and control. Most of the time this appears to work, and some modicum of control does hold the classroom together. But we can do better and can teach students how collaboration, partnership, and power sharing can create a more inclusive and democratic classroom where students might not feel like they have to confront authority to seek attention.

Disciplinary structures that are authoritarian or humiliating make it almost impossible to create a positive learning environment. Some teachers experience a constant struggle between their efforts at control and students who persistently test the established boundaries and the teacher's power. We believe a focus on relationship and a ton of patience can help teachers move away from this flawed model toward one based on human connection and building trust.

Another lesson can be drawn from the bouncing ball story. Teachers fear losing control in their classrooms. It's a perfectly normal concern, and the apparent solution is to assert even more control. But an opportunity to build trust and relationship in the classroom is then missed. As the ball bounced and the other students started getting annoyed, it became a shared problem. When Jaye bounced the ball back to the student without issuing any reprimand, the class experienced her trust that everyone in the room could eventually act appropriately.

> What has been your experience with students who challenge power—either when you were a student or as you're observing in classrooms? Can you think of a student you could look at in a different light and see some space to change your relationship with them?

Building Trust in the Classroom

Trust exists in different yet related ways in schools and classrooms.

- **The trust between teachers and their students.** Trust is the foundation for positive relationships between teachers and their students. It is developed over time and comes from teachers creating a classroom environment with clear and achievable agreements that are fairly and consistently enforced. It is based on teachers providing instruction that is relevant and engaging and making sure class time is used wisely and interestingly. Many kids automatically trust teachers because of positive school experiences and healthy self-esteem. But others don't because of their past classroom experiences, their exclusion from the dominant culture's school expectations, or their social or emotional issues. For these students, trust is hard won and takes patience and persistence to develop because it can be at odds with a student's prior, more toxic connections to school.

- **The trust teachers have that students will do what they say they will do.** For example, when a student needs to go to the bathroom, work in the school library, or get something from their locker, the teacher can trust that they will do that without unnecessary detours or violating some school rule. As instruction becomes more authentic and opportunities arise for students to go out into the community, they are trusted to do things like researching at a public library or interviewing local authorities. The trust that students are doing what they say they are doing allows this type of freedom.

- **The trust students have with one another.** It is a beautiful thing to observe a classroom where students listen to and respect one another. When students encourage and support one another, there is learning and joy. In this classroom students accept one another and each other's differing views. Students treat each other as valued learning partners.

Tips for Building Trust with Students

Be your own authentic self. Share parts of yourself and be curious about what's going on in their lives. Be welcoming without being phony.
Accept students as who they are in the moment.
Listen to hear.
If you promise something, deliver.

Laugh when things are funny or falling apart and humor seems warranted.
Be honest, consistent, and direct, and hold students accountable for their behavior choices. Avoid being punitive, and let natural consequences follow from student choices.
Be patient as students test and violate the trust you are offering in the classroom. Talk about why your trust was violated and what they can do differently next time. Make a new plan together.
Don't hold a grudge.

Probably the most important tool for building trust is patience—trust takes time to develop in the best of circumstances. Expect to be tested by students. At bottom, remember that you are the adult in the room and that your goal is to create honest and authentic relationships with your students so you can learn together. Nearly all students want to be valued and accepted for who they are. They want to be seen and encouraged. They want to engage with adults who value them as interesting and worthy partners in the learning process.

The reality is that some students are not intrinsically motivated in some or any subjects, yet we need them to persist to learn course content or practice academic skills. The trust that underlies your relationship with a student can help motivate them to struggle and push through hard tasks when they might be right on the edge of understanding or completion and want to give up. Sometimes quiet encouragement, with "I know it's hard, and you've done great so far, but do you think you could give it another try?" can help a student do their best.

Kids Will Test You!

It's our job to invite and nurture students into relationship. Some will gladly join you, which is certainly a relief. Others won't be as quick to accept your offer. As you work on detoxing those students, they will test limits and the sincerity of your offer of relationship. They will check boundaries to see the elasticity of the relationship and challenge the durability of it. And test they will! It is developmentally appropriate to test. Perhaps the hardest part of this whole relationship thing is dealing on an hourly and daily basis with this testing and still come back for more, day after day.

> I remember standing at our kitchen counter in October of the first year of New Vista. Here I was, an allegedly successful teacher with twenty years of experience, wondering whether I could do it. I was just not sure I could walk into school one more time and face the cynicism and resistance of students who rebuffed my attempts to develop positive relationships with them. I was dealing with a lot of kids who'd been burned and defeated by school up to this point. Would their aggressively passive responses, not to mention their aggressively aggressive ones, win out over my commitment to work from relationship instead of power and control? What really helped me get through moments like this was the motivation and engagement of the students who were already in relationship with us and who were strongly committed to the success of New Vista. Their trust and concern for the school and each other mattered tremendously. They supported our active learning lessons by being engaged and curious. They modeled respect for each other in a variety of ways and embraced the idea of working together in the classroom. As a colleague of ours says to students, "Do you believe that I believe you can be successful in our classroom?" They believed, which helped all of us believe.

Your patience and insistence on talking through problems might feel like a loss of power or control on your part, but gradually most students will realize that your classroom is a safe place. But not all will. You have to be OK with those students who fight against relationship. You can still offer mutual respect and maintain class agreements. You can be honest and kind and accepting of each student who spends time in your classroom and expect similar behaviors from them. You will have great connections with some students, but you may not be the right teacher for others. You can't be everything to every young person.

> What do you think are your strengths in developing trust and authenticity with your students? What fears do you have that might get in the way of relationship building?

Culturally Responsive Relationships

Because relationships are the heart of teaching and because equity, authenticity, and real-life engagement are important, we must address our roles and attitudes regarding the wide range of student backgrounds, ethnicities, cultures, and ways of being that we interact with every day. We must be willing to be vulnerable in assessing our own biases and the systemic biases in the school system to build honest relationships. Especially if you are a white teacher, this involves not being complicit in the unexamined systemic racism and unrecognized privileges many of us have unwittingly accepted and been comfortable with throughout our lives. This awareness will help build honest relationships with all our students. Our students need to hear us acknowledge there is an oppressive system that limits opportunities and discriminates, and our schools and culture perpetuate it. This is important work if we hope to close the achievement gap, promote the democratic purposes of schooling, and create equitable classrooms where all students feel safe to engage and learn.

> When I was in first grade, I chose Ramón to be my partner in a class activity. I thought he was nice, and I had a crush on him—whatever that means to a seven-year-old. I liked how his hair went up in front—flying off the right side of his head. We took hold of each other's hands and went over to the table to work. My teacher came up to me and told me in front of Ramón that I couldn't be his partner because he was "dirty." She then put Ramón with another student. I knew in the moment, even as a first grader, that what she had said was wrong. I felt terrible for Ramón. I knew what she said wasn't true. I did not trust this teacher after that.

We want every teacher and every student to feel indignant about discrimination and inequity and to speak up. No child should ever experience what Ramón did. It's our job to make sure these sorts of incidents don't happen in the first place, and it's our responsibility to get upset and intervene when we witness them. We hope white people are educated about how to be advocates and allies for children from diverse backgrounds in our schools. As teachers and as citizens, we need to examine the ways our own worldviews affect how we perceive, teach, and interact with the wide range of students we will work with. Public schools have the charge to educate all students.

For all students to be cognitively, socially, and emotionally available for learning and for teachers to successfully teach, the school must feel safe. This can only happen in classrooms where the teachers are working to be culturally inclusive, are advocates for justice, and are explicitly anti-racist. It cannot happen in a school where the staff are insensitive or unsupportive of the diversity in its community. It can't happen if a non-white teacher or staff person is disrespected and unappreciated.

> I co-taught a sociology class with another colleague. We had an amazing opportunity to focus this class on culture and diversity. It was tough dealing with the prejudice and ignorance our students revealed. On the other hand, we created several rewarding activities where we witnessed insight, humility, and a desire for activism. Most revealing was a field trip we organized where our mostly white, middle-class students did school exchanges with either a rural school or an urban school with mostly students of color. Students from these other schools then visited New Vista. The assumptions and stereotypes, the biases and prejudices, were put right out there. One New Vista boy threw up because he was so afraid to go to a predominantly African American school. Several students didn't show up that day to avoid going on the exchange. Some of the urban kids were afraid to come to Boulder because there might be bears and mountain lions. The rural school didn't seem "hick," whatever that had meant, as students had assumed. It was an eye-opening experience for all. In the debrief session, students realized the universal common culture of teenagers and appreciated the differences in each community. We had held a mirror up to their previously unexamined biases and fears.

Some of the hardest emotional and intellectual work we have ever done has involved examining our own privilege and becoming more aware of the prejudices and cultural lenses through which we have viewed the world and our classrooms. We've come to realize it's a lifelong process—painful, exciting, and transforming. As beginning teachers, we entered the profession with enthusiasm for changing the world and making it a better place. We thought we didn't discriminate because we had marched in civil rights and anti-war protests, and, after all, we're social studies teachers! We had read progressive histories and taught about oppression, reform, and social justice. We soon realized that all of this was not sufficient to form the sorts of relationships we knew were crucial for working well with all students.

Fortunately, our school, its staff, and at times the school district challenged us to examine our existing beliefs and practices. In that process, we realized the extent of the work we had to do if we wanted to engage more authentically and honestly with all our students and colleagues.

> A fellow teacher thought it would be great to show a movie about a young white man who became a hero by helping an impoverished and oppressed community of color overcome obstacles. We thought it would build on our curricular program where students did community service or explored career goals. We hoped the film might be motivational and inspiring.
>
> Sadly, it took one of the teachers of color to tell us why this movie was inappropriate. It showed a white person coming to the rescue of a community of color by solving their problems for them. It was one of those moments where we realized how much we were blinded by our socialization, bias, and cultural views. From that experience, our awareness grew, and we were on alert for similar situations of cultural appropriation and white savior stories.

Our district's equity goals created a process for learning about and listening to each person tell their stories. In that process, we learned about our own privilege and its effect on our teaching and relationships. By listening to others, we developed an awareness of how our background, color, gender, class, and ableism had molded our worldviews. We know that we still maintain elements of ourselves that are biased and racist.

Our society and our socialization immerse us in systemic racism—the source of institutional injustices such as mass incarceration, housing discrimination, and lack of equal access to quality education and health care. Until we acknowledge this, our classrooms can't be places where each student has opportunities to be successful.

As white heterosexual people, we learned a particular set of norms, values, and expectations from our family, culture, gender, and country. The way we talk, the way we interact with people, and our feelings about belonging, safety, acceptance, and self-worth are products of our upbringing and the world around us. Our worldviews and personal lenses say, "This is how we do it here." But we can't reach kids if we don't acknowledge their different lived experiences and worldviews. There are so many different forms of socialization and ways of being in the world. Students probably experience more feelings of not belonging or not being accepted than we know. Some may not love the gender they present. Some may have families that don't reflect what's considered the norm. Some don't talk or look like others around them. But they can still come together in schools to learn.

A culturally responsive teacher looks at the background and identity of each kid based on their racial, ethnic, cultural, linguistic, and class background and their gender identity and sexual orientation. That teacher is open to who the student is in the moment and who they are becoming. We are more competent when our classroom policies, pedagogy, and practices acknowledge, celebrate, nurture, and respond to each student's unique self. A culturally inclusive teacher learns about student cultures, in-group differences, and identities to make instruction more inclusive. Diversity then informs classroom management and pedagogy. The units and activities in these classrooms recognize injustice and oppression and work to make the world a better place.

We cannot highlight enough the importance of honoring and learning about all the different worldviews in our schools and classrooms. We can never fully know what images, words, and actions might appear as benign to some but as powerful or loaded reminders of oppression to others. As we become more aware, sensitive, and culturally proficient and as we listen to others' stories and histories, our students will be better able to learn and our colleagues will be better able to thrive.

Are You Being Inclusive?

Would a student walking into your classroom feel like it's a place where they belong? Who and what do they see on the walls? Do they see a diversity of faces, bodies, artwork, or symbols? Do they see quotes or signs in their native language?

Who do the students see and encounter in the halls, classrooms, and offices? Do these people reflect the diversity of the community as a whole? What do the school's hiring committees look like? Does the school have an explicit commitment to diversity in hiring?

Do students see themselves and the accomplishments of people like them in the teaching materials? Do curriculum development and textbook adoption committees make inclusion a priority?

Does the curriculum explicitly address bias based on race, gender, language, religion, culture, ableness, size, and identity? Do you introduce additional materials that bring diverse voices and perspectives into the curriculum?

Do you seek out and share novels, blogs, webpages, magazines, and TV programs that represent multiple ethnicities and cultures?

Do your curriculum and instruction disrupt the dominant white narrative by authentically addressing the history of oppression?

Being able to answer in the affirmative to these questions is a powerful way to be an active ally to every student in your classroom and school. If we don't think about these questions seriously, we will continue to misrepresent or deny the broad range of possibilities for human achievement in our teaching. Additional actions to becoming an ally include the following:

- Examine how your own upbringing, experiences, and world-views might contribute to oppression and inequity in school and take action to address them.

- Speak out when you encounter racist, sexist, ageist, classist, sizeist, homophobic, ableist, or anti-religious words or actions.

- If you are white, identify as female or male, or are North American, learn and read about how these characteristics confer privilege and may affect and limit your perspective and contribute to internalized dominance.

- Listen to friends of color, LGBTQIA+ friends, immigrant students, and others who may be different from you so you can stand with them.

How might your own background and identity hinder or help your ability to be inclusive? To be an ally?

EQUITY WORK IS A PROCESS THAT SUPPORTS RELATIONSHIPS

Equity work is crucial, but it doesn't mean students and staff will automatically feel safe with us or be open to relationship. Being on the path to becoming a culturally responsive teacher means having to be conscious of what we assume, what our life experiences and privileges have been, and what we don't know. It means working to earn trust not by trying to automatically solve problems but by listening to learn about the problems.

As teachers, we tend to believe we always must make things right for others. Becoming a culturally responsive teacher means that you first have to fix yourself by listening and learning. Your students and colleagues have things to say about their lives and experiences.

Our school's equity training included Personal Experience Panels where people talked about their lived experiences—such as being lesbian, Latina, poor, or differently abled. We listened with no discussion and no questions . . . just listening. We had one-on-one conversations, called *dyads*, on tough topics concerning all the isms of oppression. We talked and listened in a structured way so each person could really hear and be heard. We found that the number one skill in working with students, parents, colleagues, our own kids, and even our spouse is to be physically present and fully there to hear another person's story. It has enriched our lives and sometimes brought forth great pain and sadness, and it's been hard.

> Out in the schoolyard, a rope hung from a tree. A swing had once been attached to it, but it had broken earlier that winter. In a conversation, one of our Black colleagues told us that when she sees a rope in a tree, she immediately thinks of lynchings. To most of the teachers in our school, it was simply a rope in a tree, but to her it was a persistent reminder of racist hatred and violence. When the two of us, as Jewish people, see concertina wire curling across the top of a wall or a fence in an industrial area, we immediately think of concentration camps.

Making Sure All Students Feel Valued

In many schools and classrooms, there are some students that teachers or administrators simply treat better than others. Common examples are teachers who overtly or covertly privilege student athletes and student leaders or teachers who denigrate different subcultures in schools. Having privileged groups in school can lead to and normalize bullying or insensitivity to certain gender, racial, or other identities.

> The sign in the front entry of the school where we once taught reads, "Welcome to [name of school]: Home of Scholars and Athletes!"

We would read that sign when we came into this school and wonder, "What about everyone else?" Schools should never be places where certain types of students are seen and treated as better, more important, or more worthy of praise than others. Students need to know that their teachers value all students equally.

Think about your own school experiences and how different kids were treated by teachers and administrators—perhaps based on styles of dress, athletic prowess, degree of engagement, racial/ethnic origin, and so forth.

Large, traditional secondary schools are complex social institutions with social hierarchies, just like in the broader society. Think about how athletes are honored with pep rallies, decorated lockers in the hallways, and talk of tonight's game or last weekend's triumph. Kids at the margins rarely, if ever, receive this kind of attention. Students of color, students from religious minorities, female students, and kids who dress differently can easily feel less valued in our schools and even more marginalized.

If a student doesn't see themselves reflected in award ceremonies, trophy cases, or gold star bulletin boards, where do they belong in school? Will they act out to get noticed, disappear into depression, or numb themselves with drugs and alcohol?

> At New Vista, we ended each term with a school-wide experience we called Exhibition Day. Projects from various classes were presented either in a classroom setting or to the whole school in the auditorium. As teachers, we marveled at the diversity of students who were up on stage in front of all their peers, dancing (with all different body types represented), presenting a science project, showing a stop-action animated film called StickMan, or demonstrating makeup artistry. Because all classes

were based on a philosophy of full inclusion, Exhibition Day was a celebration of all types of students. We watched young people who we knew would never have had an opportunity like this in a more traditional setting being warmly and enthusiastically cheered by the whole school community.

While you might not be able to engineer an experience like this on a school-wide basis, you can still create opportunities in your own classroom to celebrate the wide range and diverse talents of the students you teach.

Because we all need to feel that we belong, kids gravitate to cliques or other groupings within the school to find that sense of belonging. There are the drama kids and the band kids and the shop kids. Kids connect around certain styles of music and/or dress. There are the stoners and the smokers, too. Kids with similar racial or ethnic identities can be seen gathered together in lunchrooms or hallways. The concern for us is not that there are self-differentiated groups of students but rather that some of these groups are valued more or less and are often treated unequally and judged by the adults in the building.

> New Vista had a nontraditional prom where all age levels could attend and having a date was not required. There was not a prom queen or king or any royalty. A male student attended in a dress for a couple of years and students saw him as the honorary prom queen. He loved the recognition and students enjoyed his clothes and presence.

Students who don't conform to certain ways of presenting themselves can be seen as threats or less worthy of relationship. When a school or teacher privileges some groups more than others, it is a travesty to our democratic foundations, denies equal access to the possibilities of our students' futures, and is a failure of relationship. It also compromises student achievement, which is the core responsibility of schools in the first place. We are not advocating a zero-sum game, where valuing all students equitably comes at the cost of appreciating any group, such as student athletes. There is room in the world of relationship to value the unique qualities of all students in the school.

> We always believed that New Vista had a disproportionately larger number of smaller boys. We're not sure if we were right or wrong, but it sure seemed that way. In our community,

there is a student "tradition" at both large high schools of throwing smaller ninth-grade boys into either a lake at one school or a nearby creek at the other school. These same kids are also more likely to be picked on and harassed in the hallways. We had a reputation at New Vista as a safe school for all sorts of students, and this sort of abuse simply wouldn't have happened there. Perhaps these smaller students who feared being victimized in high school chose to enroll at New Vista as a safer bet.

Imagine how much more ready these students were to learn and engage without the fear of being tossed into the water, pushed into a locker, or de-pantsed. Imagine if all schools were safe not only for small boys, but young Black men, smart girls, and all other kids.

Being Present in the Hallways and Public Spaces

In my sophomore year of high school, I was painfully knocked on the top of my head by a bully each day during a passing period for an entire semester. I can recall the bully's name and face and to this day I remember the feelings of frustration, humiliation, and powerlessness. No one ever intervened, and there seemed to be no way to safely report what was going on. There was no choice but to endure it until class schedules changed.

As we make our classrooms safer and more inclusive, we should have heightened awareness of our interactions with students in the larger school environment. Report after report before and after the COVID-19 pandemic reveals that significant numbers of students have been bullied, been made fun of, experienced abuse in the hallway, or been spit upon by peers. In one example, 5 percent reported being tripped, pushed, or shoved in the hallway. In a school of two thousand students, this would be one hundred students who can't move safely from one class to another. Then add in the ways that social media pressures play out among students between classes or in the lunchroom and you can see that the public spaces in schools can be challenging for students to navigate.

What was your experience of school hallways when you were young?

Teachers are justifiably busy during breaks, planning and preparing for their next period. Students seek out teachers for extra help or missed assignments at the end of class and during passing periods. Thus, adults are usually absent in most secondary hallways, aside from either official hall monitors or the teacher hurrying from one classroom to the next. Hallways in large secondary schools are a kind of no-person's-land. Kids pretty much rule in hallways—all you have to do is look at any movie or television show about high school to see that. Public spaces should be safe places for all types of students, where adults affirm and reinforce school norms about appropriate language and prevent bullying and intimidation.

For example, we had a school norm that terms such as *gay* or *fag*, when used as insults, were unacceptable, whether uttered in the classroom or hallways. One of our obligations as teachers was to be present in hallways between classes and during passing periods, as well as visiting the smoking area. We explicitly sent the message that teachers and staff would not cede authority over these common spaces and allow them to be a normless territory. When in the hallways, we'd interact with students, touch base with advisees, and generally keep an eye on student behaviors. Most importantly, when we heard a phrase like "That's so gay," we intervened to support school norms.

This intervention by teachers—and sometimes students—was usually in the form of "Hey, we don't use *gay* as an insult at our school." This was crucial for building community and relationships at the school and reinforcing basic norms. When we intervened, kids who identified as gay heard an adult affirming the inclusive norms of the school. It reminded other students that a word for one's identity shouldn't be used as an insult. Kids who might be questioning their identity heard and saw that the adults in the building were there to support them. The offending student learned directly and supportively that their language was inappropriate here. Over time, we started hearing students at New Vista say, "Hey, we don't say *x* anytime, anywhere" because over the years they expanded their sensitivity and carried social justice norms beyond the walls of the school.

When we don't name and confront any inappropriate language, kids of color, students with disabilities, young women, and gay or questioning kids learn that it really isn't safe to be themselves, regardless of what the official norms might be. The person using the offensive term learns that demeaning language is actually OK to use in the school. Kids who are questioning their sexual identity remain unsure of their safety if they decide to come out or explore their gender identity. As Desmond Tutu said, "If you are neutral in situations of injustice, you have chosen the side of the oppressor." Teachers must address all instances of discrimination and uses of pejoratives, racial slurs, sexist language, and bullying, whether in the classroom or hallways or in the world at large.

Ways to Engage in the School's Public Spaces

Chat with students about missing assignments or questions at the doorway. This allows you to see and hear what is going on around you in the halls.

Make a conscious effort to avoid isolating yourself in your classroom during passing periods, lunchtime, or other breaks in the daily schedule. Get out and interact with students and fellow staff members.

Pay attention to, listen for, and attend to student behavior when moving through the hallways.

Encourage a school-wide and staff-wide commitment to being in the hallways for the purposes of relationship and not solely as enforcers.

Ask your classes what the culture of the hallways is and address the concerns they mention.

Make yourself available in places where students don't feel safe in the hallways or elsewhere in the school.

Who Will You Be as a Teacher?

We bring our unique selves to the classroom. This reveals itself in the many adjectives students use to describe their teachers. As beginning teachers, we had to figure out how to be authentic in the classroom. How could we use our own personality to broker relationships and motivate learning? Being too nice meant students might take advantage of us, but if we were too tough, we could get into issues related to power and control. The tension between who you are and how that plays out in the classroom while getting kids to learn is a struggle most new teachers confront. It's something every teacher has to struggle with when starting a new school year with all new students. Understanding who *you* are is a part of building relationships.

> What kind of teacher would you like your students to characterize you as and why? Funny, weird, hard, friendly, easy, cool, nice, challenging, interesting, great . . . something else?

We found we could maintain our personality and develop honest relationships when we figured out how to be what we think of as "hard teachers." Judith Kleinfeld describes this as being a "warm demander." A hard teacher or warm demander can be funny, friendly, cool, weird, and nice. They have high, but appropriate, expectations for all students while being deeply committed to relationships with them. This teacher communicates that each student can keep doing better and can excel beyond their current levels of learning. Hard teachers are teachers who push because they know they've put supports and structures in place to encourage students to the next level of achievement. They know the balance between pushing just enough and pushing to levels of frustration and stress. Because relationship is central, hard teachers balance interpersonal connection and emotional support with encouragement to keep going a little further academically or socially. Students know that a warm demander or hard teacher cares about them in authentic ways, even as standards of rigor are expected and upheld.

Being an effective teacher means having "caring inflexibility" in the face of constant student pressure to accept late papers or otherwise bend rules or expectations. This is the teacher who, according to student chatter, is really demanding but also engaging and caring and who really helps them learn. This teacher holds students accountable when they mess up and have to face the consequences but also offers solid emotional support. Students learn that this teacher is also nice! It's a balance and a tension at the heart of relationship-based teaching in genuine ways.

Some students with lower self-esteem or fear of failure may be afraid of a hard or warm demanding teacher. That is why it is so important to have that friendly face, the greetings at the door, the encouragement that the student can do it, and the classroom agreements that tell every student they are welcome here. Many students who have been marginalized in school do better with a teacher and classroom that emphasizes acceptance, allows expression of feelings, builds community, and has high and achievable expectations.

Table 1.2. Different ways of being the best teacher

Successful hard teacher behaviors	Behaviors where hard is hurtful
• Bring humor and a sense of lightness to interactions with students • Believe in students with positive, unconditional regard • Enforce clear boundaries without rancor or belittling • Communicate that each student can meet course expectations and provide the support needed to learn • Be persistently positive and optimistic to encourage student motivation • Hold students accountable when they mess up and have to face the consequences of their actions • Show compassion when kids' lives are hard • Show flexibility when circumstances are unusual	• Be excessively strict without explanation • Set unfair or opaque grading expectations or boundaries • Offer limited opportunities to get a good grade or to demonstrate learning • Set expectations that are essentially unattainable • Put AP or other test scores and their own reputation over student needs • Control students through fear and intimidation • Treat some students better than others • Be critical without making room for improvement • Use scare tactics for control • Use name calling, humiliation, and sarcasm

Another way to characterize what we're describing is being *firm* and *friendly*. This means setting and maintaining clear expectations and engaging authentically with students. New teachers wrestle with balancing expectations for behavior with wanting to be liked. It's a learning curve. There is a huge difference between being friendly and trying to be friends with your students. It's not our job to be our students' friends. Lots of kids may like you, but do they respect you? After taking your class, will they feel that they grew emotionally and interpersonally and learned important skills and content? A young teacher can use the closeness in age to their students as leverage to push them to excel, but it is a delicate dance.

Over the course of our careers, we came to believe that one of the highest compliments a teacher could receive was to be described by a student as "my hardest teacher and my favorite teacher."

What term fits your goal of the teacher you want to be: a good teacher, a hard teacher, a warm demander? Some other descriptors? What does that term mean to you?

Maintaining Boundaries

A critical part of developing positive relationships with students is creating and maintaining appropriate boundaries with them. We just pointed out how it's easy as a young teacher to fall into the trap of wanting to be a friend to their students—which is very different from being friendly. Students will respect you for having limits and boundaries because they need someone to be the adult in the relationship. They have plenty of friends, but they may not have a lot of positive role models. That is what you should be.

There is no need for teachers to share most aspects of their social lives with their students. If you live in the same community as the school where you teach, students may see you in your out-of-school existence, and that's fine—although we remain amazed at how startling it is for some kids to see their teacher in the grocery store. Sharing interests like music, woodworking, biking, or poetry is perfectly fine and can serve as positive modeling for students and a way to connect. But recounting stories of parties or favorite craft beers has no place in healthy teacher-student relationships.

Calling students inappropriate names crosses what should be a boundary of mutual respect between you and your students. If you call a student a name out of anger or frustration, you need to figure out why you lost control. You need to think about why you would belittle a student. It may be intended as a joke or sarcasm, but we never know whether our comments are received as funny or hurtful. There is no room for a teacher to ridicule a student in any way. You are the adult—the role model paid by the community to act appropriately when interacting with students.

In my fourth year as a teacher, I was asked to oversee an independent study program for a middle school student. This student was very bright but also cocky and a handful to deal with. In a conference one day, I insulted him. The next day I heard from his mom and I dutifully apologized, although there was really nothing to say aside from "I was wrong, and I'm sorry I disrespected your son." I ran into this student about thirty years later at a community event. We said hello and then he reminded me how I had insulted him. Thirty years later, that insult was still fresh in his mind.

It's also hard to defend swearing in the classroom. In our minds, the classroom is hallowed ground: a place of high energy but also decorum and manners. It is a place of learning, not a private space or a reality TV show. Swearing is inappropriate. Students may laugh, but it's not the way to have students relate to you. In fact, some students will be disappointed in you. A slip or a mistake is one thing but swearing as part of your regular instruction is inconsiderate, ill mannered, and not what we want to model for students.

How you dress can affect the classroom atmosphere and is another case of where you should establish appropriate boundaries between you and your students. We've worked with some teachers who think that if they dress like their students, the students will relate to them better. It doesn't really work that way. You're an adult, and that won't change by trying to look like your students. Dress in ways that show respect for the profession.

Another place to be clear about boundaries is online and in social media. Be intentional about what you post and with whom you interact. Norms continue to shift around what might or might not be appropriate and, at some level, you are modeling for your students. The positive side of this is that you can be aware of and help students negotiate their social media interactions. Much happens outside of class, but knowing students well can help you know if a student is facing online bullying or dealing with online comments that are hurtful or being misunderstood. Help students know the risks of sharing inappropriate images and how to be safe when online. Don't ignore the social pressures that students face interacting online and through social media.

It is important to maintain clear boundaries around sharing your own religious and political beliefs. It's fine for students to know that you are interested in politics or that you attend a particular place of worship. But the sharing of specific political opinions crosses a boundary because students should be able to come to their own conclusions about political affairs. We are hired to teach, not to advocate on partisan issues. The same holds true for individual religious beliefs. It's fine for students to know that you do or don't adhere to a specific religious faith, but you have to maintain a solid boundary around any efforts to proselytize. Schools are one of the most important places for a clear separation between church and state.

Some of our colleagues disagree with us on whether teachers should share their political views. Some research says it is important to do so, especially in the higher grades where students may already be voting. Students can benefit from a teacher sharing their political views as a way to model the thinking process of coming to a position on a controversial public issue. Certainly, a teacher playing devil's advocate enhances the democratic process of hearing all sides before making a reasoned opinion. We explore this in more depth in chapter 4 when we talk about teaching controversial issues.

Again, we prefer to have students develop their own opinions because we may unduly influence those opinions. Also, for new teachers with untested discussion skills it could be a murky ground between inculcating one's views and expressing one's views. As teachers become more skilled, they may use their own reasoning as a good example of how to think critically.

What you can and should do is stand up for broad universal and democratic values. When conflicts arise between a family's values and school norms of inclusion and equity, we must stand up. If a student says, "My family or priest says being transgendered is wrong," it is important to say, "Some religions or families have strong feelings about this, but everyone is welcome and safe at our school and in this classroom." You can acknowledge that there might be a broad range of values in the community around topics like sexual identity, politics, or religion, but the school has norms of equity and inclusion for all.

It's the same idea as when a kid says, "My mom says if someone hits me, I should hit them back." That's a value that conflicts with school values of relationship and nonviolent conflict resolution. As teachers, we don't tell the kid their mom is wrong, but we tell them that at school we solve problems in a different way. It is a way to not step on the values of the family and uphold safe boundaries at school.

What Do You Say about Drugs and Alcohol?

When we came of age as teachers, we expected students to ask about our own drug use in high school and college. Talk about boundaries! It was the early 1970s, and secondary students in those years wanted to know what we had done when we were around their age. We were both in our early twenties, and John was teaching in a school with only eleventh and twelfth graders. He was only four years older than the seniors. Needless to say, kids were curious and pushed on this issue. Our stance then and now was that either answer, yes or no, would be unhelpful to our students and corrosive to our relationships with them. If we said yes, we could be seen as sanctioning teen drug use, which we certainly didn't want to do. If we said no, many students would have thought we were being untruthful. They would have shied away from a relationship with a teacher they suspected was being dishonest. Instead, we told students that this was our own personal history. We were also quite forceful in communicating that we believed adolescent drug use is unhealthy, unproductive for growing minds, and illegal. The same held true when they asked us about drinking alcohol.

As we write this, there has been a sea change in societal attitudes toward marijuana use, with increasingly widespread acceptance of medical and social uses of pot. What's a teacher to do now? We suggest taking that same stance. Where marijuana is legal, your decision to use or not use it is a personal one and doesn't need to be shared with students. Although alcohol was legal at age eighteen when we were young teachers, we never shared our own experiences with drinking. Instead, we helped students understand the consequences of inappropriate drinking, such as impaired driving and nonconsensual sex, and we urged good decision making and following the law. We believe that boundaries like these help students see teachers as role models who think, engage, question, and participate in their own communities.

Beware of Silencing Student Voices

Early in my career, I thought that my views on politics and social issues were the right answers to the world's problems. I was going to end injustices, bring world peace, and end poverty by educating the next generation of change agents. I taught my own political views and violated the boundaries we are now advocating. I didn't have the pre-service training or the knowledge about teaching controversial issues to know that what I was doing wasn't right. Because I was eager to become a better teacher and was invested in my own professional development, I attended lots of conferences and workshops. I gained new tools for conducting true class discussions and open-ended activities. I learned how to encourage students to take different positions and look for the best arguments on each side. I was now teaching instead of advocating. It became heartbreakingly obvious how wrong I was in my earlier assumptions when I ran into a former student long after he had been in my class. He told me he had loved my class, but that I had created an environment during discussions where he felt that his opinions, which were different from mine, would not be heard safely. I had silenced his voice in the classroom. I felt horrible.

Who knows what legacy of other silenced students we left behind in our early years of teaching. This was not a situation like the one where the student said his family thought being transgendered is wrong. Because society has moved forward and accepts different gender identities as normative, now is a time to clearly support school norms and expectations of equality and inclusion. In Jaye's situation, she didn't allow space for students to express viewpoints different from her own in classroom discussions of controversial topics such as the Vietnam War. She lost many opportunities to educate instead of indoctrinate.

It is our obligation to help students explore the whole spectrum of political beliefs without feeling silenced by one teacher's opinions. This is the way to prepare young adults to be open minded and critically aware citizens in a democratic society. And because public schools are secular in nature, we also need to keep our own views on religion and non-religion out of our classroom. There is nothing better than watching students try to figure out what they think you believe and hearing them argue with one another about what they think your position is on a political issue. It's fascinating and rewarding.

Reflect on the various boundaries we've highlighted. With which do you agree or disagree or question? Are there others you think are important?

The Trap of Overemphasizing Content

When asked what they do for a living, many secondary teachers say, "I teach math" or "I teach history," with an emphasis on their particular content area. There's nothing wrong with this, but an overemphasis on content can get in the way of our commitment to nurturing relationships.

Content isn't the enemy. In fact, it's at the very heart of our jobs. Unfortunately, the pressures of teaching content often result in less attention being paid to the hard work and time commitment necessary for creating and nurturing relationships. Elementary and middle schools are pressured to teach to high-stakes tests. High schools are explicitly preparing most students for postsecondary education, and content takes on increasing prominence in teachers' planning and instruction. Testing, coverage of content, huge class loads, and the ever-looming anxiety of college admissions tend to increase pressure on teachers, some of whom come to see relationships as either a luxury or "not really my job." We have more to say about this in subsequent chapters.

There are many areas in high schools where relationships blossom. Drama teachers, music teachers, and coaches build excellent programs based on relationships. Some of the most successful math, science, arts, social studies, and language arts teachers find ways to build strong relationships with all students while teaching interesting content. Our experience, however, is that these were the exceptions and not the rule in most of the schools in which we taught or mentored.

A school that values relationship can still have a challenging academic program and prepare students for the real world. At New Vista, where relationships were a priority, our students were admitted into competitive colleges and universities, as well as a wide array of professions that don't require a college education. They became skilled artists and writers, project managers, musicians, teachers, programmers, and entrepreneurs. Relationships helped students know themselves better and act on what was important to them. Relationship was crucial for boosting all students' levels of achievement and self-worth.

How Our Own School Experiences Can Get in the Way

Prospective teachers come into teacher education programs having spent thousands of hours as students, watching teachers teach. Education researcher Dan Lortie calls this the *apprenticeship of observation*. From elementary school through college, most of us experienced instruction dominated by lectures and textbooks. Teacher-student interactions were structured around power and control instead of relationship. These become the default models when pre-service teachers begin teaching. They just haven't had many experiences with active and engaged learning or classroom management based on authentic relationships. What we advocate in this book is even more challenging to implement if you haven't experienced these types of classrooms in your own schooling. Without alternative models, we revert to what is most familiar from our own apprenticeship of observation.

One of our biggest challenges working with student teachers was pushing them to see that students can learn in the more interactive ways we describe in the next chapters. They couldn't visualize it because they hadn't experienced student-centered instruction when they were in school. The good news is that many more prospective teachers have experienced more innovative models of teaching.

The apprenticeship of observation also affects how we envision teacher-student relationships. We advocate the centrality of authentic relationships between teachers and their students without teachers ceding their authority in the classroom. There is shared power in that students have responsibilities, choice, and agency. The teacher is there to help students learn. In these classrooms, the teacher's primary responsibility is to come to know their students well and use that knowledge to enhance instruction and achievement. Classroom management becomes dominated by conversation and shared problem solving. Students have a voice in both how the classroom is conducted and discussions about course content. But it is hard to do this if you have no lived experience of it.

Describe your own apprenticeship of observation. What challenges will you face as a teacher in overcoming it? Or, if your apprenticeship of observation was positive, describe it.

Making Relationships Central to Your Teaching

If you make it a priority to develop deep and authentic relationships with students, you'll be able to find time for it. Yes, a teacher's day is a blur of responsibilities and activity. Secondary school teachers are responsible for more people than most managers in the business world; the quick pace of class periods and passing periods would make a non-teacher's head spin. Elementary school teachers juggle schedules for art, music, and physical education and the responsibility for teaching multiple disciplines in one class. When you add the rollout of lessons, management of daily administrative demands, and handling of unruly students, we really are on our toes all day long.

Sometimes we miss cues from some of our students. It might be "Pay me more attention because I did the homework for the first time" or "Don't call on me because I didn't do the assignment because my parents were fighting all night" or "Please ignore me because I'm high and I don't want to get busted." Whatever is going on and regardless of how busy our day, it's important to be aware of what a student's behavior is telling us about them as individuals and to check in.

> Being high school teachers, we drew from a huge pool of students to find babysitters for our kids, and several of our students became beloved sitters. One was a quiet young woman, incredibly responsible and hardworking, who really liked school. She never missed class, she got good grades, and was a good student. Sometime during the school year, her parents decided to divorce, and it devastated her. She now had more family responsibilities and was sad and depressed about her parents' breakup. Her attendance fell off and her schoolwork declined. Because we knew her well, both in and out of the classroom, we were there to support her in any way we could.
>
> A few months later, she confided in us that not one teacher or adult at school had noticed or said anything to her about her increased absences and drop in grades. This only increased her despair. We were saddened as well. Here was a good student, quiet and responsible, who didn't make waves. Yet not one teacher out of six during that semester had connected with her about her change in behavior or grades. After having her home life upended, she felt aban-

doned and unsupported at school. Aside from us, no teacher had taken the time to develop a meaningful relationship with her.

This is a perfect example of how the lack of relationship can affect a student. Be that teacher who says, "Hey, what's up? Let's talk."

Chapter 2

Managing the Classroom with Relationships

Building and maintaining positive relationships with students helps create the environment where students can thrive academically and socially. Classrooms must be safe for ideas to be expressed and all voices to be heard if students are to learn. Managing the behaviors and climate of the classroom requires effective classroom management skills.

What you'll find in this chapter:

- Why we use *classroom management* instead of *discipline*

- How to establish and use classroom agreements when building a classroom management system

- How to devote the first week to teaching students how to learn in your classroom

- The concept of *student as worker* in your classroom

- How to use conversation to manage and improve student behavior

- Understanding student behavior as a form of communication

- Why anger and shouting aren't useful for managing student behavior

- The importance of developing a sense of *with-it-ness* as you interact with the class and individual students

We use the term *classroom management* instead of *discipline*. Teachers are in the business of managing classrooms, both instructionally and behaviorally, to create environments where learning is central. Teachers have the authority to create the workspace and climate of the classroom, as well as to establish agreements about the standards of behavior and accountability with students. Effective teachers do not try to dominate or control students. The term *discipline* has a punitive feel when you are trying to put relationship at the forefront of your interactions with students.

Students want structure and boundaries in the classroom. Few students are comfortable in chaotic classrooms, but that doesn't mean that some won't try to create chaos or get into power struggles. Boundaries are likely to be tested over and over.

> One of our first junior high school principals grew up on a farm. He told the story of how young calves, when first let out into a fenced yard, would invariably run around looking for an opening to escape. When they found one, they would shoot out and need to be rounded up. Back in the enclosure, they would run directly for that same opening hoping to get out again. He said students are just like young calves, testing our limits and pushing against our boundaries. When they find openings in our classroom management systems, they head straight for them to see what they can get away with.

Effective classroom managers establish boundaries to make sure the learning enclosure is large enough for exploration but secure enough for consistency and security. The use of agreements to establish boundaries in the classroom provides room to explore and yet maintains expectations for behaviors that keep everyone safe and able to work and learn.

It takes practice, patience, and persistence to develop the confidence to use your relationships with students for classroom management instead of relying on teacher power and authority. Managing a classroom filled with a diverse group of students is complicated, to say the least. And it takes time and experience to deal with the wide range of things students will do in the classroom. This is where it is important to know your students and use that goodwill to work with them. Be good to yourself as you gradually develop more and more management expertise. Just because today was hard doesn't mean that tomorrow can't be better.

Non-educators with content expertise are often encouraged to become teachers. The idea is that these experts, without teacher training, can be brought into schools to improve student achievement. We feel this reveals a general disrespect for the skills and expertise required for teaching and a lack of awareness that students need more than content from a teacher. After teaching all day without tools for managing student behavior, is it any surprise most of these non-educators soon end up quitting?

In Which Classroom Would You Look Forward to Learning?

Classroom A: First day of class, students come in and sit down. The teacher welcomes everyone and reorganizes students into seats alphabetically by last name. The syllabus is passed out and the teacher reads it aloud, noting the required school supplies, behavior rules and consequences, and important upcoming dates. The teacher distributes textbooks and then launches into a lecture-style overview of the course.

Classroom B: First day of class, students come in and sit down. The teacher has students pair up and introduce themselves to each other and find two things they have in common. Students are then given a brainstorm task to complete together. The pairs of students share out their ideas, which are posted on the board. After being given another prompt, the pairs return to talk about the new information. Back in the large group, the teacher summarizes the information the students generated and explains why they did the activity, stressing that they want the students to know each other, work well together, and be actively involved in the class. The teacher then hands out the syllabus for students to look at as homework.

Think of the differences in these two classrooms and the roles of the student and teacher. In classroom A, the teacher stands in front of the students telling them what to do, students are passive, and there is little interaction. In classroom B, students are thinking and interacting with each other, and the teacher is facilitating the activity. Students are starting to get to know each other, and the teacher is learning about the students. We hope you think classroom B looks like the more interesting classroom in which to teach and learn. What goes on the first day starts building the relationships that support classroom management.

Starting at the Beginning:
Establishing Classroom Agreements

The first step in creating a classroom that is designed for learning where students respect each other, feel safe, and work well together is to establish classroom behavior agreements. Some people use different words like norms, behavior contracts, or classroom rules but we prefer the word *agreement*. These agreements are statements of expected behavior and attitudes that are accepted and practiced by the members of a class. The term agreement refers to mutually agreed upon behavior expectations and ways of interacting in the classroom. These classroom agreements need to be established whenever you begin a new class with a new group of students.

Establishing these agreements takes time and occupies much of the first few class periods, and it happens in tandem with helping students experience how they will learn in your classroom. Begin by asking, What frustrates you about learning in school? What behaviors get in the way of your learning? What bothers you about working in small groups, participating in a discussion, or getting your work done? This sets up the expectation that the classroom behavior agreements will help remedy their frustrations. It also gets buy-in from the students because they come up with some of the problems the norms should address. This discussion demonstrates that you care about their concerns and will work with them to make the classroom a safe and productive space.

After this initial discussion, create a list of agreements and present them to the class for discussion and clarification, making sure they address the concerns students listed, as well as *your* needs as the teacher. Agreements should be clear, brief, and to the point and should clearly state appropriate behaviors. They are best stated positively whenever possible, and the list should be relatively short, usually no more than five items. Extensive lists of agreements or expectations can be overwhelming and lead students to start finding loopholes or cracks in the system.

Present the list of agreements and get student feedback on them. Do any of the agreements seem unrealistic or unclear? Go around the room and ask each student if they can accept the agreements. If yes, that's great. If not, pause to determine the problem and try to resolve it. If it can't be resolved, ask if the student can at least live with the agreement. Or suggest that they try the agreement for the coming week and then the class can reevaluate. This may be a place where some students want to test boundaries. By revisiting an agreement later, everyone can save face, and by then you may have won over some contrarians. During the week, check in with those who had a problem with the agreements and see how they are doing.

Listing of agreements is not enough. Structure conversations about what behaviors the agreements imply and how to recognize and practice them. If an agreement states, "Respect each other's property and person," discuss how students would go about respecting someone else's property and person. Brainstorm examples and counterexamples. Make sure to post the agreements prominently in the room for all to see and so you can easily refer to them when necessary. Refer to the agreements when things are going well and explain to students that this is because they are contributing positively to the common welfare of the classroom.

Five Suggested Classroom Agreements

Respect each other's identity, person, property, and ideas.
Be on time for class and prepared for the day's lesson.
Be kind and use appropriate language.
Listen to understand.
Bring an open mind and curiosity to our shared learning.

A culturally responsive teacher relies on behavioral agreements to create a safe place to learn and support all different types of learners, including those who have faced racism, sexism, homophobia, sizeism, or other forms of disrespect in school. Students who are shy, are fearful of not knowing enough English, or are being bullied may be hesitant to participate in a classroom without supportive agreements. Having and enforcing agreements means that conversations and relationships can be based on respect and every voice is valued. If students don't have to worry about survival, they can have fun appropriately and the freedom to explore who they are and what they want to learn. Students have shared responsibility for the safety of the classroom and a sense of true belonging.

> Do you remember behavior agreements, or some sort of rules being posted in your classrooms in school? How safe did you feel in various classrooms as you moved through your years of schooling?

The power of classroom agreements arises not out of your announcing and posting them but in your careful and consistent use of them. Enforcing agreements is much easier when they are clear and you are willing to hold students accountable for their behaviors and choices. Challenges to agreements can be handled without shutting students down. Here are a few examples:

- If a student uses inappropriate language, stop the activity or discussion and refer to the agreement by saying, "Thanks for contributing, but let's remember that one of our agreements is to use appropriate language. How else could you express that?"

- If students aren't listening to each other in a discussion, stop what you're doing. Ask the class what agreement is being violated at that moment. In this case, it might be not respecting the ideas of others. It could be that students aren't being open to opposing ideas. Ask how the present discussion would be different if the agreements were being followed. Move on with a clear statement that the agreements are important for positive interactions in the classroom.

- If you have an agreement about being on time, hold kids accountable for being on time. If you don't hold students accountable for lateness, then why should students pay attention to the other agreements? When they come in to make up time during lunch period or after school, use that time to fortify the relationship, find out why they are having trouble getting to class on time, and make a plan for the next time they are tardy.

Enforcement of rules and classroom agreements needs to be done in the context of the growing relationships you're working to develop in the classroom. Sometimes it's OK for a student to make a mistake without excessive penalty. As students challenge classroom agreements, try to balance being firm and being friendly by using humor and being good natured. This early part of the school year, when the boundaries are being tested, is when students figure out whether you really intend to enforce positive classroom behavior.

If a student is persistently disrespectful and if humor or other minimal interventions haven't worked, it's time to take them aside at an appropriate time and have a conversation about what's going on for them and what needs to change. When a student is pestering another classmate, intervene gently and firmly in the moment and remind them to respect each other's space. Later, be sure to check in with both parties to see if things are improving or to see what's going on.

Tell the class that you are accountable for following the agreements too. If students are expected to be at class on time, you need to start instruction when the bell rings. Be sure that respect works in both directions.

The First Week:
Practicing and Modeling Agreements and Expectations

The first week of school is a busy one. Schedules are getting revised and finalized. Students are finding their way through the hallways. If you're a new teacher, you're doing the same! Despite what might look and feel like chaos, the first days and weeks are your opportunity to teach and model how learning will take place in your classroom.

During the first week, it's important to have students practice how they will work in your class. Small-group work and small-group discussions are central to the classroom environment and pedagogy we advocate. Students don't necessarily come into a classroom with the skills and experiences to engage in worthwhile discussions or work appropriately in small groups. Students need to learn how to listen to diverse voices and opinions, how to have an open mind, and much, much more.

Many teachers start the first day by reviewing the course syllabus, sharing classroom rules or expectations, and launching right into the course content. School has started and time's a wasting! Instead, you'll be well rewarded if you invest time and energy in the first week so your students can get used to the ways you intend for them to learn together. This is very important for, among others, non-majority students, second language learners, and students with learning plans to support them in understanding the culture and requirements of your classroom.

Students who have had years of learning in more traditional paradigms or are not part of the dominant culture may require explicit teaching and practice to be able to work in small groups and find their voice in discussions. Students who have relied on the teacher and textbook to provide the content need to experience how small-group work distributes meaning making and intellectual work among students, with the teacher off center stage. From the very beginning, students need to practice learning how to think instead of having the teacher tell them what to think. This is another part of the detoxing process we described in chapter 1.

Too often, students view small groups as a time to take a break and rely on other students to do the work for them. When given an opportunity to discuss a topic in small groups, it's common to hear, after barely a minute or so, "We're done," or to hear nothing at all. Most students lack experience participating in and moving a discussion along to explore an idea in greater depth or diversity of opinion. These skills must be explicitly taught, modeled, and practiced from the very first day. Classroom activities will sink into a pit of inertia unless all students are committed to participating and being valuable contributors in the learning environment.

Going Slow to Go Fast

You might worry that taking instructional time to teach small-group skills, practice small-group discussions, and reinforce classroom agreements takes precious time away from covering content. But experts in classroom management have shown that taking time to help students be successful in using the strategies and procedures we employ in our classrooms actually allows more time for focusing on content over the course of the year. It's worth "going slow to go fast" by front-loading modeling and practicing how you do things in your classroom. This is especially true for ensuring that small-group work is a productive learning experience.

Creating a Successful Classroom: Day 1

Here's one way to begin the first day as students settle into the room and before going over the syllabus or even the classroom agreements.

- Quickly identify partners. The easiest way is for neighbors to work together. Give them a moment to briefly introduce themselves.

- Tell students that their task is to brainstorm all the reasons the course content might be useful or valuable to them and/ or society at large.

- Give simple, clear instructions about how to brainstorm. The goal is to come up with as many ideas as possible, avoid judging contributions, and think creatively.

- Tell pairs that both students should write down all the ideas they come up with and that you expect at least seven distinct ideas.

- When everyone is ready, tell students to begin brainstorming and allow them two minutes to create their lists.

- As they work, wander around to make sure students are on task and to encourage further thinking.

- Stop the brainstorming after two minutes and, with the whole class contributing, begin recording information on the board. Solicit ideas from a wide range of students—they all have lists in front of them! Use this as a time to start learning names.

- After all the ideas are on the board, return students to their pairings and ask them to spend thirty seconds discussing which reason on the board they think is most important.

- Return to the large group, sample student choices, and explore them in greater depth.

A lot happened during this short activity! Instead of telling students that their voices would be important in the classroom and droning on about rules and course outcomes, you modeled making student voices central from the very beginning of class. You also began shaping learning expectations in small groups by having students practice *being* in small groups. The activity started small—only a few minutes and in pairs—so there were few opportunities for students to avoid the work and the task was easy to accomplish, which minimized frustration and allowed everyone to contribute. Students probably behaved well without your having to begin with a whole list of classroom rules because on the first day most students try to do the right thing. Part of teaching from relationship is starting with a "presumption of innocence"—assuming that students can and will appropriately engage in a learning activity.

Use the remainder of the class period to develop and discuss classroom agreements, as described earlier. You can refer back to the short activity for examples of what the agreements might look and sound like. Reviewing the course syllabus can be homework or can wait for the next day. In this single class period, you've started teaching students how they'll learn in your classroom, and you've begun the process of establishing relationships and modeling classroom agreements.

> The first lesson may not always go as expected. At the start of a course called African History and Literature, I initiated a brainstorming activity and was posting responses when a student raised his hand and asked, in a way that was clearly intended to challenge me, "As a white teacher, how can you teach about Africa?" This was a gutsy question for the first half-hour of a new class. The rest of the students were immediately engaged, waiting to see how I would respond. Despite having taught for about twenty-five years, my pulse quickened. I took a breath, paused, and then politely asked, "What makes you ask that question?" He was a bit taken aback by my not pouncing on him, but he explained that he thought that as a white teacher, I couldn't have any real understanding of what it meant to be African. I listened and asked the class what they thought about this assertion. Lots of students had things to say, and we had an interesting discussion about whether someone could teach about something they had not personally experienced. The whole interaction probably took twenty minutes, at which point I ended the discussion. I asked the original student if he had anything to add. He wasn't totally satisfied, but he really didn't have much more to say. Then we returned to the brainstorming activity.

What everyone learned in this episode was unconnected to African history and literature, and maybe more important. The student who asked the question seemed to be staking a claim as a classroom provocateur by testing the teacher. Perhaps his behavior was communicating some sort of mistrust. When the question was treated respectfully and not as a challenge to authority, he and the class saw that his question was worth discussing and, more importantly, that the teacher wasn't going to respond to a power play with another power play. The student's question was honored, other student voices were engaged, and everyone experienced working together productively at the very start of the class. Without getting defensive, I shared my thoughts on his good question. We have more to say later about these sorts of interactions when we talk about *behavior is communication.*

What are your thoughts, and maybe fears, about students challenging your authority in the classroom? How could you reframe those situations and turn them into learning opportunities?

Day 2

For the next class period, find some item of course content that lends itself to small-group work and discussion. It might be a quotation in literature or a short, interesting paragraph for students to read and discuss. It might be a current event or an ethical issue in science. It could be an interesting statistic from the daily news or a piece of art in an art class.

This mini lesson plan provides an example of how to give students more practice working in groups and using classroom agreements.

As students come into the classroom, have desks arranged in groups of four or enlist help in moving the furniture before defining the task. Groups of four work well because the desks can face each other, creating a focused working space. If you have tables and chairs, move them so you have groups of four distributed around the room.

Remind students about the basic classroom agreements that were discussed the previous day and are now posted on the wall. Share your expectation that the agreements will be helpful as they work.

Before explaining the task, have a whole-class discussion about how to work productively in a small group. Ask them what helps make small-group discussions productive and what gets in the way. Write these on the board in two columns. Spend time exploring which obstacles to productive small-group discussions are the most bothersome and what to do about them.

Practice phrases that help small groups be more productive, such as "I'm interested in what Amelia has to say . . ." or "Let's each give our opinion first before coming up with the solution . . ." or "Miguel, what are you thinking?" Brainstorm any other pitfalls of small groups and add them to the list on the board. Chat about how to avoid them. Model appropriate body language for small-group work and perhaps even exaggerate a poor example.

Tell students they will be unable to finish the task before time is up and that you expect them to work until you say "Stop, please." We'll explain this stopping technique a little later in the chapter.

Explain the small-group task and get them started. Make this first small group work only three to four minutes in length. Over time, you can gradually extend the time that students work in small groups. As students work, circulate and listen to the conversations. Show them you're valuing what they're doing while listening for appropriate behaviors.

After you stop the small groups, get the attention of the whole class and report out what they discussed. One way to do this is to get one contribution from each group as you go around the room instead of having each group give all their thinking at once. When reporting out to the large group, there is no need to rearrange desks. Students can turn in any direction they need to in order to participate. You should move around the room, standing by different groups.

First review the content of the small-group work with the whole class and then reflect on and critique the small-group process. What did they do well, and what needs improvement for tomorrow? Ask to hear from everyone before anyone speaks twice. This is especially important early in the year when you are helping students learn how to be effective in small groups and find their voice in the large group.

The lesson plan we just described is very detailed and structured and it needs to be. The structure combines your energy to build relationships with specific moves to positively engage students. With practice, small groups can become engaged, efficient, and productive, but it takes planning and commitment. At the end of the class is the time to review the syllabus. Students will be much more interested in where you are taking this class now than if you had started talking about the syllabus on the first day.

Shared Expectations for Effective Small-Group Discussions

These will complement your class agreements. Don't be afraid to model them and have fun acting out positive and negative behaviors.

We enjoy talking with and learning from our classmates.

We listen to understand, extend, inquire, and clarify.

We ask questions to help ourselves and other group members extend discussions.

Be curious and make connections between new and old learning.

Body language and demeanor should communicate engaged listening and respect.

It's our conversation and learning, not a performance for a grade.

Each of us has a voice and is invited to speak and share. No one is excluded!

We all push the group's thinking together.

Speak thoughtfully by avoiding "and stuff" or "blah, blah."

Everyone in the group cares about everyone else's learning.

Getting the Attention of the Class When You Need It

In classrooms where students are actively engaged in learning, things can get loud and you need a way to get the attention of the class without repeatedly shouting. You can explain the following management tool to students on the first day, when you are discussing agreements, or you can just use it when you first need it during the first week.

FIRST: In a clear, loud voice, say "Stop, please!" once. Wait a couple of moments—maybe count to five silently.

NEXT: Again, say "Stop, please" once. Wait and count to five silently again as the noise begins to subside.

THEN: Say it one more time. The class should be focused on you by this point.

The first "Stop, please!" alerts the class that something is changing. Some students will stop what they're doing and pay attention to you. This will change the tone and volume in the classroom perceptibly. The second "Stop, please!" reinforces that it's time to attend to the teacher;

more students will start paying attention. The final "Stop, please!" allows those last couple of students who have to say just one more thing to finish up. It honors the fact that these students still had something to say. Now you can give your next instructions to the class.

Another technique is to say "If you can hear me, clap once" (pause for a moment). "If you can hear me, clap twice" (pause). "If you are quiet, clap three times." This brings the class back to attention without shouting. Another prompt to get attention might be "Eyes on me!" You can also use a system of counting down from five to one. This honors student voice by letting kids finish whatever they are saying. When you reach one, it's your time and they should be paying attention to you.

Elementary school teachers have imaginative ways to get students to listen. One teacher put on a hat when she wanted her kids to pay attention and all the kids would start saying to each other "the hat, the hat" and be quiet. What strategies might you develop for the students you'll be teaching?

Day 3

By the third day, you have the beginnings of a classroom culture for engaged learning; you're practicing classroom agreements of inclusion, respect, participation, and doing real work; and you're creating relationships with students by greeting them at the door, checking in on them when you see them in the hallways, and watching and listening to learn how each one ticks. A teacher's life is busy, to say the least!

On this day, you might want to continue working with small groups by giving students a short, interesting reading from the course content. It could be something on cloning, a brief historical dilemma, a choice faced by a character in literature, or a playground dilemma. Pick something interesting, but avoid highly contentious topics that are likely, at this point, to be overly polarizing. Students don't yet have the skills to work with such issues, and that is not your intent here. Your goal is to set up an interesting conversation, not provoke a heated argument.

Think about how you'd adapt the plan below to fit the content you'll be teaching.

- Give students time to read the passage or read it aloud to them if there is a wide range of reading abilities or language fluency among the students. One of the benefits of reading the text aloud is that everyone is finished at the same time! When finished, ask students to write down a position and one good reason for that position. Do this before moving into small-group work to model thinking before discussion.

- Explain that the task in small groups is to come up with a list of all the possible pros and cons in the dilemma or controversy. As always, remind the class of the norms and how they practiced working in small groups in the last lesson. Ask every student to record the responses generated in the small group. Limit the task to three to five minutes. It's much better if kids complain that they don't have enough time rather than they have too much time to get off task and start chatting about their social lives.

- After you call time, have small groups report out the pros and cons to the large group as you post them on the board. Clarify them as needed. Then, return the discussion to the small groups, with the goal of each group considering all the pros and cons, trying to reach consensus on how to resolve the dilemma or address the controversy.

- After four to seven minutes, return to the large group to share positions and see if the class as a whole can come to any agreement. If so, that's fine. If not, what are the central points of contention? Allow each student to develop to their own conclusions as they listen to various arguments and positions. Before concluding the discussion, spend time specifically highlighting the most compelling arguments on both sides and try to identify places where all sides might agree. This models the important skill for citizens in a democratic society of working together to find common ground rather than encouraging further polarization.

- The lesson could end with a short writing assignment that serves as a diagnostic of student writing skills.

Sometimes small groups just won't get down to work or the students will seem unable to work together. You can address the situation with gentle persistence and by communicating that this assignment isn't going away and neither are you! Often, teachers get frustrated with students who act inappropriately in small groups and decide not to use this format. But this takes away the opportunity for students to practice the skills they need most. Students might feel like they've won, but they've only convinced their teacher to take away a potentially engaging and important learning opportunity.

If a group is having a problem getting to work, kneel down and ask what's going on. See if you can determine the source of the issue. Listen but also communicate that now is a time for them to work together on the assigned task. Get them started by asking one of the students to contribute an idea. Make sure everyone writes it down. Move to a second student and do the same. Remind them of the classroom norms and communicate your belief that they can do this successfully. If several groups are having the same problems, you might need to stop the activity and begin a conversation with the class about why they're not engaging in the assigned work. Check to see if there is confusion or a lack of clarity about the task. We'll have more to say about this later.

As the first week proceeds, continue to reinforce classroom agreements as you use and model small-group and classroom discussion skills. (Chapter 4 goes into more detail about how to do this.) Teach and practice the ways you expect students to participate in instructional activities. Make sure small-group tasks are based on ideas and issues that students will find interesting, and gradually increase the time allotted for small-group work. When you are delivering content, find ways to insert worthwhile small-group time so students can interact with the content.

As the school year progresses and pressure builds to cover more and more content, maintain your commitment to allowing time for discussions, small groups, and engaging instruction. As needed, remind students how to behave in small groups and participate in high-quality discussions. Continue to teach, model, and practice the classroom agreements.

Students as Workers: Shifting the Cognitive Load

A common phrase in education and one we value refers to the *student as worker*. Regardless of grade level, it should be the students who do the bulk of the intellectual work and make meaning in our classrooms. This means that students are *inquirers* and *producers* in classrooms. These terms imply that learning begins with student curiosity and results in some sort of tangible product.

Students who are workers, inquirers, and producers are less motivated to misbehave and have fewer opportunities to do so. Lessons that require students to interact, think, analyze, synthesize, create, and evaluate are meaningful work so there are fewer reasons to goof around. As student engagement goes up, management concerns go down.

> I was hired to teach US history, but I had taken only one or two US history courses in college and none that directly connected to what I was expected to teach. I tried to read as much as I could ahead of my students, but I soon realized that there was another way to deal with this situation. I began to figure out ways for my students to do the learning of the course content instead of my doing it for them and presenting it in lectures. I used jigsaw learning strategies where different groups of students researched topics and shared what they'd learned with others. I did mini research projects that produced posters instead of papers so students could do gallery walks to learn course information. In essence, I was having the students be the workers as I stayed enough ahead to be able to help and support them. It's one of the reasons I value these sorts of student-centered instructional strategies. As a new teacher, unsure about my background content knowledge, this made a huge difference in how I approached my job.

Unfortunately, in most classrooms the teacher does the bulk of the intellectual work—researching and synthesizing information to present in lectures and writing questions for tests and quizzes. In classrooms dominated by direct instruction, students passively absorb carefully curated information and feed it back on test day. Many students become adept at taking notes, filling in worksheets, and memorizing whatever is on this week's test or quiz. This is work, but not meaningful intellectual work. Higher-order thinking and the creation of original insights are missing. Equally important, it's easy for students in these classroom settings to misbehave, whether out of boredom or spite.

We had a high school colleague who repeated this sequence week after week:

- Monday: lecturing to introduce the week's chapter, distributing worksheets for the chapter's content, and giving the class time to start working

- Tuesday: showing a movie or other visual presentation on the chapter content

- Wednesday: giving a lecture

- Thursday: allowing individual work and study time

- Friday: giving a publisher-created test on the chapter

This routine went on for the entire school year. One day before winter break, a student came to our shared office and asked our colleague for all the third-quarter worksheets. He said he had a lot of free time over the holidays and wanted to get a head start on the worksheets.

We don't need rote memorization in an age of smartphones and computers. We need thinking and communication skills. The sort of instruction described above offers no opportunities for stronger students to be challenged or for choice in how or what students learn. Think of how many people associate history with boring readings and mindless worksheets because that was what they did in social studies for years on end. How many don't like reading because a teacher told them what was important about the book. Many kids don't like math because of never ending worksheets. A student who is a worker makes sense of content rather than just finding it in chapter text and recording it on worksheets, whether paper or electronic.

What are your memories of lectures and worksheets vs. more engaging instructional strategies when you were in school? Were you a *worker* as we've just described? Did you want to be?

When students are workers, inquirers, and producers, they use and practice these sorts of skills:

- Finding patterns among facts and data

- Figuring out relationships of cause and effect

- Making connections between course content and the world outside the classroom

- Wrestling with historical, literary, scientific, or other sorts of dilemmas

- Being curious and asking their own questions to go deeper into content

- Listening to and taking seriously differing points of view

- Creating new insights or ways of thinking

- Using primary sources to help answer questions

- Convincing peers of their position on a controversial issue

- Thinking and problem solving like historians, writers, scientists, mathematicians, and others

When planning and delivering instruction, we should strive to make the work students do as purposeful and engaging as possible, both for the short term and for lifelong learning. When given interesting and worthwhile academic tasks, most students engage and do the work willingly. Misbehavior tends to be reduced.

Here are examples of instructional activities where students are workers, inquirers, and producers:

- Socratic seminars, which are text-based, teacher-facilitated discussions that involve authentic conversation and meaning making

- Project learning that demonstrates student understanding of mathematical concepts

- Role-playing activities in which students model real-life interactions

- Structured Academic Controversies (SACs), which are cooperative learning-based discussions of different perspectives on controversial topics

- Simulations in which students become historical, literary, or scientific figures and think like those people

- Poster projects or slideshows where students display their understanding of content for others to learn from

- Original video productions, such as turning a short story into a movie or creating a short documentary

- Writing letters to the editor or creating political cartoons, public service announcements, historical journals, or newspapers and magazines

- Using geographic data sources and technology to analyze and hypothesize about topics such as pandemics, plastic pollution, or human migration

- Engaging in oral histories of family members or others in the community to learn history from a more personal perspective

Integrating these strategies into your teaching repertoire may take more time to create, plan, and structure, but they shift the work in the classroom to the students, where it belongs. You can learn more about these sorts of instructional strategies online or from colleagues. Over our career we developed a wide menu of choices like these for students to choose from and with each new strategy, we broadened the options we could provide to students. We explain more about this sort of planning in chapter 3.

These engaging instructional activities have the added benefit of reducing behavior issues. Students are busy—often too busy to be off task. The tasks have purpose, which builds motivation to engage and stay engaged. Few students have an active intent to misbehave in class. Rote learning and purposeless instruction provide them with opportunities to act out. Look around at most staff meetings and you'll see that your colleagues are often no better at staying focused when the meetings drone on.

Behavior Is a Form of Communication

Despite all your efforts to establish and model your classroom expectations, there is still the nitty gritty of dealing with inappropriate student behaviors. Even if you've used the first week to establish agreements, develop relationships with students, and provide ways for them to be the workers in your classroom and use their voice, some kids will misbehave. They may talk out of turn or chat with neighbors. They may ignore your directions or challenge assignments. They may be defiant. This is inevitable—and a source of frustration and anxiety for any teacher, new or experienced. It's important to step back and ask what's going on with a student for them to choose to misbehave. What are the social and emotional issues behind the student's behavior?

Behavior is a form of communication. A student's actions are telling you something about what is going on in their heart and in their head—even if they don't know what. When there is outright defiance or persistent efforts to get attention negatively, it's time to think: What is this student trying to say to me? Why are they making this choice? What is going on behind the behavior? When you ask questions like this instead of automatically instituting consequences, you begin to examine what might be motivating the behavior you observe.

We rarely ask why things are going well when a group of students happily work on a project together. But if we were to look at what that behavior is communicating, it would tell us these kids are feeling OK, know what is required, feel valued in the classroom and by the teacher, and are doing something interesting and engaging. Negative behaviors tell us a different story. Whether it is a kid pushing other kids on the playground or a middle schooler lying about an assignment or a high schooler falling asleep at their desk, it is telling you that something is awry.

This is the time to talk to the student, get help from the counseling staff, or connect with other colleagues who might know the student better. Try to find out what is going in this student's life. It might feel like the time to meet student defiance with your authority as the teacher, but nothing could be further from the truth. This is when you need to do your very best to listen to and hear the student and to show that you care about them as a person beyond whatever behaviors they're presenting in class. While it is so very hard, avoid anything that might feel like escalation. It's a time to show caring and compassion. It's time to focus on relationship.

Imagine what might be going on for a young person that would make open rebelliousness seem like a worthwhile or effective tactic. The behavior might be a manifestation of pain or prior school experiences. It might come from years of racial discrimination or feeling different, unaccepted, or unsuccessful in school. Some behavior problems in the classroom come from students having given up on learning. Their self-esteem is built up only when they succeed in bugging the teacher or gaining negative attention. Their behavior is saying, "I'm going to avoid feeling bad about myself as a learner by showing I am a good troublemaker."

Some negative behaviors might be a result of an altercation with parents before coming to school. Teacher threats of greater punishment only help validate whatever anger or disconnect the student is already feeling. Don't play to the student's expectations in your response. Calm listening and caring can be the most disarming of approaches and allow for the beginning of some sort of dialogue. In these situations, it's best to try and do no harm. Respect, relationship, and trust all argue for increasing the listening and compassion rather than the opposite.

Here are some questions to ask to turn negative attention-seeking behavior around:

- Can you tell me what you are feeling? Tell me more.

- What do you want out of this class? What are you doing to get what you want?

- Is what you are doing working? If it's not working, can you think of something that will?

- What do you have to do to get through school and on with life?

- Can we explore some ideas to help you?

The result of this interchange could be that the student formulates a goal or plan and an action to take. If they are successful, celebrate the success; if not, make a new plan. A classic aphorism is "plans fail, not people." It is important to make the student aware that they are in charge of their behavior. It's not their mom, or friends, or the weather; it is them. When students blame things outside their own control, they lose their own agency to solve the problem. We have to help students take responsibility for their choices and actions. And we have to start in ways that are not punitive.

Using Conversation to Manage Behavior Choices

Given that behavior is communication, conversation is one of the most effective tools for classroom management. You want to explore what is preventing a student from engaging in learning. Conversation is far more effective than shouting or getting angry, and it's a management strategy that arises out of and reinforces relationships with students. Nearly all issues, whether behavioral or instructional, can be resolved through conversation. Of course, there are students with certain disabilities and other diverse needs for whom more structured responses and systems are called for. But for most students and situations, conversation can be one of the most effective and humane problem-solving approaches in your management toolbox.

Several attributes of conversation make it a powerful and effective way to deal with management issues in the classroom. Conversation is low impact. It doesn't immediately escalate an issue into a power struggle and leaves plenty of room for alternative strategies. Conversation also supports the relationships that are at the heart of being an effective teacher. By saying to a student, "We need to talk about this," you are making clear that the problem resides somewhere between you and the student. This helps avoid an immediately defensive reaction from the student. Problem solving through conversation begins with the statement "What can *we* do *together* to resolve this situation?" instead of what *you*, the student, need to do differently. This promotes a more collaborative approach to problem solving.

Conversation as a management tool is based on the idea that it takes time to change behaviors instead of expecting them to change in an instant. When you have an authentic conversation with a student you are telling them that you care about them beyond the immediate incident. Having a problem-solving conversation takes practice but the format and content remain the same.

TEACHER: Thanks for taking some of your lunch period to talk with me. I've noticed that you have a lot of things to contribute to class discussions. Would you agree?

STUDENT: I guess . . . I like to talk in class.

TEACHER: I also notice that you tend to shout out answers when other kids are trying to speak. It seems hard for you to wait your turn. Do you notice that too?

STUDENT: I guess . . . but they're usually done talking.

TEACHER: Actually, what I see is your excitement to say something without always listening to what another student might be saying. That's a problem. Our agreements are pretty clear about respecting the ideas of others and listening to them. My job is to balance every student's desire to speak and be heard. So what can we come up with together to help you participate more appropriately during discussions?

STUDENT: I don't know. If I have something to say, I should be able to say it. You said sharing our ideas is important in your class. I have things other kids should listen to.

TEACHER: That's true, but this is about sharing the limited space we have for all students to get their voice in discussions. Again, what could you do differently that still lets you have voice without stepping on the ideas of others? And is there something you'd like me to do differently?

STUDENT: I guess I could wait sometimes . . . yeah, I could maybe just sit back now and then. And maybe you could just call on me once in a while?

TEACHER: That's a great start, and it would be really helpful. How about this: What if in the next discussion, you get four times to speak. I'll count, but I'll expect you to keep track too. After four times, I'll ask you to hold your comment back. Could you do that? And if I call on you, that won't count as one of the four times.

STUDENT: Maybe. But what if I have something really important I want to say? Are you saying that after four I just have to shut up?

TEACHER: Yeah, that's what I'm suggesting. Maybe you could be more careful in deciding when you want your voice in the discussion. Maybe you could write down something you want to say so you don't have to say it out loud. Maybe you could challenge yourself to keep one of the four times in reserve just in case you want to say something at the very end. I think you can do this. Will you?

STUDENT: I suppose . . . but what happens if I don't stick to the four?

TEACHER: I suppose I'll try to ask you to hold back during the discussion and we'll meet again to revise this plan or come up with a different one. Maybe we'll agree that you should be an observer during the next discussion so you can see what the discussion is like without your voice. You have interesting things to contribute to our discussions, and I really want your voice in them. But I also want you to learn to think a bit more before you contribute, to make your contributions carry more weight, and to listen more to what your classmates are saying. It might help you become a better listener. I want you to succeed. OK?

STUDENT: I guess . . . are we done yet?

TEACHER: Almost. Just to review, in the next class discussion you'll work to keep your contributions to a maximum of four times. Right?

STUDENT: OK. Can I go now?

When you brainstorm and suggest strategies, the student becomes a collaborator in moving forward rather than the object of punitive action. There certainly can be consequences for not following a plan or for being consistently outside of established classroom agreements. But consequences that are created through conversation are more powerful and compelling because the student has a degree of buy-in to the solution. This should be clear in the conversation. In fact, part of the conversation should be about the planned consequences for not changing inappropriate behaviors or doing as agreed.

Here is another place where authenticity is important. If your classroom agreements are to be more than just something posted on the wall, your conversations around management issues need to be grounded in them. The give and take has to be real, and any negotiation over possible consequences should be honest and authentic. As teachers, we have to listen and have the flexibility to entertain consequences we might not have initially considered. We also get to communicate our bottom lines. When the discussion is honest and the consequences have student buy-in, the odds of behavior change increase dramatically. It can't be a sham process for telling a student how they need to act and what they need to do.

Conversations with students can take place during lunch, after school, or any time that is convenient for both you and the student. In addition to dealing with whatever created the need to meet, it can also be an opportunity to build connections. Deal with the issue, but also just talk and spend time getting to know the student better. We know a teacher's time is precious and losing planning or grading time for behavior issues is exasperating, but this is a perfect situation in which to build relationship. Maybe that student won't need to take up more of your time later.

There are many reasons that some students might find it challenging to collaborate with their teacher in a one-on-one problem-solving conversation. Cultural values associated with respect and deference to the authority of the teacher can make it uncomfortable for them to contribute to a conversation like the one we've just described. Language proficiency issues may call for the services of a translator to make sure the nuances of the conversation are not lost. A history of discrimination in schools and classrooms can make it hard to collaborate with others. When you know your students well, you can make plans to ensure that conversations with them can be culturally sensitive and productive. In addition to building community with all students, you are helping them better understand how the culture of your classroom operates. They are also practicing skills that have value outside of school.

Conversation is also a powerful tool for addressing whole-class behavior issues. Instead of shouting or issuing threats, get the attention of the class, remind them of the classroom agreements, and begin a conversation with them about whatever is going on. It's the group's problem, so the conversation is with the class as a whole. Classroom agreements guide the discussion, with an expectation that students will speak respectfully and listen intently.

Try this process:

- Begin with "We need to stop for a moment. We're not listening to each other, and people are shouting to be heard [or whatever is the issue] and not following our class agreements. What's going on, and what needs to change?" Listen to the students' views.

- Ask how they can act differently to follow the class agreements. If students are talking over each other, for example, your conversation can focus on why that is disrespectful of the classroom agreements and what needs to change.

- Review the agreements and list specific ways to work together productively.

- Get the commitment of the class to practice appropriate behaviors before moving on.

- Before the bell rings, take time to reflect with the class on whether and how behavior improved. If so, that's great. If not, then what's the plan for tomorrow?

There are any number of reasons why the class feels like it is falling apart. A class might be acting out because the directions aren't clear. Students might want more choice in the work you assigned or how to complete it. They might find the work boring or not see the purpose in doing it. They might be overly engaged and ignoring agreements. Students have insights into what is happening in the classroom, and a savvy teacher will pay attention to what they have to say with genuine curiosity. Listen, make a plan together, and then be sure to carefully monitor and follow up with the class. As in working with individual students, relationship and trust are at the heart of the process. Only in a classroom where those two elements are present can there be authentic problem-solving conversations.

There are few, if any, quick fixes for dealing with classroom management issues. It takes conversation after conversation to help shape and mold student behaviors. It takes time and patience with failed plans and ineffective consequences. Whatever behaviors are being addressed didn't develop overnight and it will take time to remediate them. By engaging in conversation after conversation, you are modeling the power of collaborative problem solving. You are working for authentic changes in behaviors rather than mere compliance. Changing behavior is scary and puts the student in new and unfamiliar territory. They need your support and the support of their peers. Ongoing discussion and conversation provide the structure and support for the desired changes. So can a good sense of humor and finding the good in whatever is going on.

> What are some of the benefits and challenges you see of using conversation to deal with classroom management problems?

When Inappropriate Behavior Continues

What do you do when a student won't participate in these conversations or sabotages them? The good news is that students who are developing relationships and trust with their teacher are less likely to take this sort of defiant stand. Yet it will happen, especially near the beginning of the year as students are detoxing from prior school experiences. Some students have a history of toxic interactions with adults in school, and they are used to acting in ways that perpetuate that toxicity. Some students have learned that the only attention they can get from adults in school is negative attention, which can be better than no attention at all. These kids are saying something to us through their inappropriate behaviors. Our responsibility as teachers who value relationship is to listen and help them learn new ways of behaving in school.

Outright defiance and breaking of agreements are incredibly anxiety producing for all teachers. It almost triggers a fight-or-flight response, and neither is appropriate in a classroom. As a first step, try to pause and take a deep breath, even as all eyes in the classroom are focused on you, waiting to see what you will do.

Here are some options:

- In as even a tone as possible, say, "Emily, that's not appropriate in this classroom. Please stop." Wait a moment and then, hopefully, return to the lesson.

- If one individual is acting inappropriately or doesn't stop when asked, tell the class to continue with their work. Go over to that student and politely ask them to come with you to a corner of the room or into the hallway. Keep calm and ask what's going on for them. Plainly and as respectfully as possible state that what they're doing is not appropriate in the classroom—for example, "When you shout out while I'm listening to another student, it makes it really hard for me to concentrate and for that student to be heard respectfully. It also doesn't respect our agreements." Or "You know you can't call another student an offensive name." Try to get a commitment of changed behavior, thank them, and return to the room and carry on with the lesson. You'll need to connect with this student after class to follow up and develop any new behavior parameters. Try your best not to escalate the situation by getting angry.

- If the whole class is acting out, as calmly as possible call the class to order (remember "Stop, please!") and ask for quiet. It might take a moment, but some kids who are acting appropriately will quiet down first. This might not be the time for a conversation. Instead, identify the problem, refer to the classroom agreements, and state what you expect the class to do differently. If they start working more appropriately, great. Appreciate the improved behavior! Then, about ten minutes before the bell, take a deep breath and have a classroom conversation about the misbehavior and develop a plan for things to improve tomorrow.

- Sometimes it is just an off day. Students are unfocused, there is general malaise, and things aren't going well. Stop the activity or discussion and acknowledge that it is a tough day and that students will now work individually. Don't be angry or petulant. It just is the situation. Whatever you are discussing, students can write their answers, or the activity can go on tomorrow. Maybe for today students can do research or read while you plan for tomorrow. The loss of interaction and having to do a less compelling task can help recommit students to the interactions they get to participate in regularly. We usually have a backup ready such as reading a poem or reading about a current event if a change in plans is needed. Having that in your back pocket will help when the inevitable bad day comes along.

Patience, persistence, not rising to the bait, and having yet another conversation with a new plan and a new set of agreed upon consequences are the best ways to manage behavior. Keep asking questions about what's going on for the individual or the class and listen to what they say. Tell students, even when they are misbehaving, that you believe in them and know they can do the right thing. In nearly every case, students treated with this sort of respect gradually come around and improve their behavior. They don't necessarily become perfect angels, but the beginning of a relationship forms the basis for more constructive behaviors over time. Some kids do dramatically change how they behave in classrooms once they experience, and come to trust, the respect they are given by teachers who they once saw as adversaries. How cool is that?

I had a student who seemed to just barely tolerate me. He was in my advisory, which was like a homeroom that met daily for differing amounts of time. Kids were with the same advisor for their entire high school career. It was where they learned how to develop and maintain long-term, productive relationships with an adult. This kid was persistently late, and he hated that I enforced consequences for his tardiness. He was sullen and wouldn't engage in advisory activities. He distracted others when I was trying to accomplish some task. We were at perpetual loggerheads. I'm not sure how much I actually liked him at that point, but my job was to be his advisor and work with him, just as I worked with other students. When he was a sophomore, he and his parents arranged a meeting with the principal to try to get him transferred out of my advisory. He said he couldn't relate to me. His parents said he needed another teacher who understood him. Following school policy, the principal denied the request and we were encouraged to work together to improve the situation.

I patiently and frustratedly worked with him and he, grudgingly, with me. Later that year, things started to improve. I still held him accountable for his behavior choices, but we found things to laugh about at other times. His tardiness became something the whole advisory noted and chuckled about. He also just got older and more mature. By senior year, he and I developed a really positive relationship. As I held my boundaries, he continued to test them but also accomplished the things he was required to do. He successfully graduated and now has a terrific career. We are in touch today and truly like each other and our shared history.

Most relationships with students, like Rome, aren't built in a day!

Dealing with Persistent Misbehavior

If behaviors that violate classroom agreements and expectations persist, you might want to get in touch with the student's family and explain the situation, describe your interventions, and ask if they can contribute to solving the problem from the home point of view. First check in with counselors and administrators to see what they know about the dynamics in the family and whether the family is likely to be helpful in solving the problem. Counselors and administrators can also support you if a family is hard to work with. (In chapter 6, we talk in more detail about how developing relationships with parents makes dealing with behavior problems easier.)

Sometimes schools have policies that mandate certain responses to inappropriate student behavior, such as suspension for a particular offense. Suspension is a complicated response to inappropriate behavior. Sending a student home doesn't really address underlying causes and issues. Regardless, classroom teachers can reduce the likelihood of these sorts of consequences by working to build relationships with disruptive students so problems don't escalate to that level. If they do lead to such consequences, we need to move on and redouble our efforts to build and maintain relationships to minimize the chances that this will happen in the future.

Helping Students Take Responsibility for Their Actions

You help students take responsibility for their behaviors when you pay more attention to what they do instead of what they say. Many students, especially by the secondary grades, are really good at making excuses and saying what teachers want to hear. They have creative explanations and great language for their various screwups and missed assignments. We had a student who always used the excuse of some family medical emergency when he didn't do assignments. He lived with his mom, and he would say she needed to go to the doctor or she had fallen down the stairs. He came to class once without his work because, he claimed, he had skin cancer and had just had it removed! It was really only a scratch on his scalp. Whether it's "The dog ate my homework" or "I couldn't access the file on the class website," there is always a seemingly plausible excuse for not completing work or bringing it to class.

We have to listen to what students say with a healthy balance of acceptance and skepticism. Fighting over excuses and having to decide which are more or less credible is corrosive to good relationships and doesn't support students taking responsibility for their actions and choices. Calmly discussing actual behavior without assigning blame or motive is much less fraught. Students behave as they do for many reasons, and our job as teachers is to help make improving their choices part of the broader learning in our classroom.

Addressing the actual behavior (remember that behavior is communication) instead of the excuse is the most effective way to hold students accountable without getting into a power struggle. Despite what a student might *say* ("I really want to succeed," "I really want a good grade," "This is really important to me"), what did they actually *do*? "Did you turn in the work or not?" This helps you not get into an argument with the student. When a student says they didn't mean to be late, the response is a calm "But you were late." There is no need to berate or browbeat them. Describe what they did and any consequence. You can do this and still show concern for the student by saying, "I know you'll try to make different choices tomorrow."

One way to help students learn to take responsibility is captured by the phrase "Bummer for you." The message is simple: what has happened is certainly a bummer for the person to whom it happened, but it isn't necessarily a bummer for anyone else. The phrase helps to situate the problem where it belongs, with the student. When used in the classroom, it needs to be stated in a caring, non-sarcastic way that communicates "Something crummy happened and it's a bummer . . . but it's a bummer for you and not for me, the teacher, so what can you do about it?"

As the teacher, we don't have to own the student's problems, but we can help them take responsibility for those problems as productively and positively as possible. Used with students in a genuine, but emotionally flat manner, "Bummer for you" helps students who want the problem to be located anywhere but with themselves know that they have a problem.

"I forgot my assignment at home . . . can I get it to you tomorrow?" Bummer for you. It *is* a bummer! No one likes to forget a responsibility and have to face the attendant consequences. We'd all like to have an infinite number of passes when we miss a deadline or fail to accomplish something. But life doesn't work like that.

Fortunately, nothing missed, not turned in, or not accomplished at school is literally earth shattering. You didn't bring your assignment and there will be some sort of consequence. That's a bummer . . . for you. I, as your teacher, still value you, care about you, and believe you're capable of meeting the next expectation and ultimately succeeding. It's just that for this assignment on this day, you get to accept the consequences. There's something powerful about being honest with students and helping them locate responsibility where it belongs—with them. Solid teacher-student relationships survive these small tests and might even be strengthened because the teacher has communicated that the student can and will do better the next time.

John's students were so used to hearing "Bummer for you" that it became a sort of mantra in his classes. Said in his friendly, sincerely sorry-for-you tone, kids knew and understood its meaning. Jaye, however, could never use that phrase. It didn't fit who she was. She might say, "Really? Tell me more." Or "I'm sorry about that, but it was due and now it's late." Or "Oh no. That's terrible." The natural consequence still would occur, and this was a way to be sensitive while holding the student accountable for the deadline or tardiness or whatever.

New teachers have to develop this skill so students know they have messed up, there are consequences, and you still like and have confidence in them. Find a phrase to use repeatedly so kids know you are serious and that they will have to face the consequences of a choice they made. One suggestion might be, "That sounds difficult/hard/frustrating/sad. What will you do about it? What will you do next time?" Acknowledge the error of the student's ways with a heavy dose of empathy. As exasperating as another late assignment or missing homework or late arrival to class is, it's an inevitable part of a teacher's life. A thick skin, consistency, humor, and kindness are all effective tools here.

Meaningful Ways to Support Students

Student social, emotional, and academic growth can be enhanced by a supportive teacher-student relationship and an engaging and challenging curriculum. If a student does well in school, they feel good about themselves. Think about the student who says, "I hate math because I'm not good at it" or "I'm not a good writer." These attitudes inhibit the learning process and reinforce negative beliefs about themselves as a learner.

There are lots of ways to honestly support students so they can begin to make better choices about their behavior in class and get to learning:

- Helping students accomplish interesting work

- Holding students accountable for high and attainable expectations and helping them get there

- Working with students through the revision process until they can, in fact, accomplish the assignment

- Providing meaningful positive attention on a regular basis

- Giving helpful and specific feedback on assignments

Avoid mindless, hollow praise. Students know it's insincere, and it doesn't motivate because it comes across as inauthentic. Link praise to something specific the student has accomplished. When students hear things like "That's interesting" or "That's a good idea" from peers in a discussion, that also supports their sense of self.

Sincere positive attention for students being who they are, for following classroom agreements, for doing their work well, and for showing up at school when it might be tough is a powerful classroom management tool. Be intentional about adding positive attention on a regular basis to your daily interactions with students in and out of class. Make a mental note of who has been off your radar for a bit, who you think has been slacking lately, who you forget to call on because they can be so quiet. Make sure those actively seeking attention get it in positive ways and those who want to remain unseen are noticed by you. As you pay positive attention to students individually and as a class, you are helping to prevent the need to intervene when they seek attention inappropriately.

Here are more ways to give positive attention to students:

- Say hi to kids when they walk into class and say goodbye at the end by acknowledging something they did well during the period.

- Notice a student who is doodling or drawing in a notebook and appreciate it. Ask what a kid is listening to on their headphones.

- Notice if a kid is interested in comics or video games or loves cats and say something about it.

- Pay attention to sports, drama, musical, and other performance schedules so you can wish them well or ask how things went.

- Learn about the wide range of student events in or out of school and offer words of interest and encouragement.

- Recognize a particularly good piece of work, even if it isn't perfect. What did the student do well or that made you smile?

- Recognize student efforts with a nod, wink, thumbs up, note, or comment.

When we ask a student about their day or about their interests, we are showing that we see them as unique individuals with interests both in and out of class. If a kid says they aren't having such a great day, be honored that they're sharing something of themselves. Find out why and offer to explore options to help make things different. Both show and act your concern! A student's behavior may be based on an issue at home or at school that requires attention before the student can be present as a learner in your classroom.

> A student came to first period and just seemed off when she entered the room. I asked what was up, but she was vague and seemed bothered. I had gotten to know her pretty well and sensed something was wrong. I put my arm around her shoulder and gently asked her to follow me. As we walked to the counseling office, I told her I was worried about her and hoped that talking to a counselor might help. I found a counselor and explained that something was troubling the student. It turns out she had come to school to say goodbye to friends before planning to go home and commit suicide.

While this is an extreme example, it shows that knowing students well and just paying attention helps us recognize when something is off. That recognition might lead to a conversation or insight that helps students move forward in their day or access other school resources. The emotional lives of students are complex, fluid, and often far more important than your teaching activity for the day. You wouldn't make a student with a broken leg sit quietly through class without first attending to the break, so don't let kids with broken emotions get ignored and be expected to just get to work. You can be that teacher who actually cares about students while you're easing your classroom management burdens. It's a win-win process.

Reflect on what you see as the balance between your job as a teacher of content and supporting student social and emotional growth.

Why Anger and Shouting Aren't Useful

The best way to manage classrooms is with a smile on your face and goodwill in your heart. There's no need to get angry, shout, or threaten to flunk the entire class. There's also no reason to take student misbehavior personally. Taking on the emotional burden of our students' successes or screwups is misplaced and not helpful. Keep in mind that the relationships you are building, nurturing, and holding to account are in service of student learning and growth. There will always be a necessary distance, even within the most positive and productive relationships with your students.

When teachers shout at their classes as a whole or at individual students, they are most likely escalating the situation, which rarely ends well. In power struggles, a teacher might win in the official or institutional sense but lose a great deal in the eyes of their students. Students will fight to maintain a sense of their own dignity, even at the peril of greater punishment or consequences. Everyone loses in these situations.

Shouting doesn't have much impact anyway, apart from the initial bewilderment or surprise. Continued shouting becomes part of the aural landscape that's easy to ignore. At some point, it's like crying wolf: When is the shouted message really important and when is it just another expression of teacher frustration? We're not talking here about the momentary, loud "Can you keep it down, please? or when a class needs to be brought to attention for a change in directions. We're talking about shouting as a means of discipline or norm reinforcement.

What you are modeling when you shout is problematic. Do we want to model for students that the way to change a situation or improve it is to be the loudest voice in the room? Unfortunately, it's not always easy keeping an even disposition when dealing with a room full of students. Early in our careers, we got angry at students for not following our norms or expectations. It was as if by not doing the work or misbehaving, they were personally attacking *us*. We pretty quickly learned that we just aren't that important in the lives of our students.

We then began to experiment with other ways of handling management issues. We attended in-service workshops on different classroom management systems and found them mostly too authoritarian or too cutesy. We finally arrived at our own system, the one based in relationship and conversation that you've been reading about in this book.

How you use your voice sets the tone for the classroom. There is a way to project your voice so students can hear you without it seeming like you are desperately trying to get their attention. Listen to a PE teacher or drama teacher and hear how the sound is supported by the diaphragm. Ask for help developing this if you feel you can't do it. Your voice can have authority without sounding mean. Sometimes changing your volume can even be effective. Try a stage whisper and see what that does.

Never Demean a Student–Ever

A fundamental rule when managing classrooms and dealing with student behaviors is to never demean, put down, or otherwise ridicule a student. The same is true for using sarcasm or humor that might be hurtful. We've heard too many stories of teachers, perhaps frustrated themselves, telling a student they just aren't smart enough to do the work as a motivation or management tool. In what universe might this be useful in the teaching and learning process? Nothing positive can come from putting down a student, whether in private or in front of their peers. Doing so might be a show of power, but it's power inappropriately held and used. Needless to say, it doesn't help build relationship. Our job is to support student self-esteem in real and authentic ways.

When students become more and more engaged in authentic and worthwhile tasks, they need stronger prompts to pay attention to directions or change what they are doing. Isn't it great that the focus and tasks are so engaging that it's difficult to get their attention?

With-It-Ness: Putting It All Together to Manage the Classroom

Classrooms can be amazingly complex and confusing places, especially for novice teachers. There is a constant stream of inputs that need to be processed and managed. These include student behaviors and misbehaviors, make-up work for students who were absent, forms to complete, attendance to take, tasks to be noted on the board, learning materials to set up, texts from parents and emails from administrators, and more. It's in this environment that teachers also need to deal with all that arises in the classroom when trying to teach effectively and engagingly.

Jacob Kounin coined the term *with-it-ness* to characterize the ways that effective teachers are aware of and deal with all the many things going on in the classroom at the same time. It specifically refers to the kind of multitasking that experienced teachers do as they perceive what's happening in all parts of the room while giving directions and also prompting an individual student to stay on task. It's like having eyes in the back of your head and the ability to hear a student swear under their breath at fifty paces, all at the same time. When you develop sufficient with-it-ness to be aware of what's going on all over the room, you can prevent small things from getting out of control and more effectively turn your focus to the higher-priority instructional demands of the moment.

One way of thinking about with-it-ness is to recall learning how to drive a car. For many of us, when we were first getting behind the wheel, it took all our concentration just to keep the car within the lines and avoid obvious obstacles. For some, even the radio was too much distraction. With practice and experience, most of us now do much of our driving almost automatically. We can (but perhaps shouldn't!) eat a sandwich and manipulate a cup of coffee and carry on a conversation all while negotiating our way through traffic signals and around other cars. With time and practice, what seemed like sensory overload became automatic and less stressful. The same is true of classroom management.

As teachers become more skilled and more comfortable in the classroom, their sense of with-it-ness grows. If you've been in the classroom for more than a year or two, compare your current level of awareness with the level you had when you were interning or student teaching. This is important because as teacher with-it-ness increases, so do opportunities to intervene appropriately when management issues arise. In fact, the greater the with-it-ness, the fewer the number of off-task or disengaged students.

A teacher who has with-it-ness can be in the middle of a lesson, notice a couple of students starting to goof around in the corner, and casually wander over and stand next to them all while continuing to address the class. The management issue is handled without having to shout across the classroom and disrupt everyone or stop the lesson. Students are amazed that you actually heard their complaint or comment so quietly whispered to a peer! With-it-ness is as close to a superpower as teachers will ever get.

Being Realistic about Classroom Management

Regardless of how with-it you might be, one of the things to recognize and make peace with is that students will sometimes get away with things. No teacher, no matter how with-it, can see and attend to every infraction or behavior outside the expected norms. Nor is it healthy or wise to try and attain this standard of control. Knowing when to pick your battles and to confront inappropriate behavior is more of an art than a science, and it develops over time with practice.

That said, one of the most important times to intervene and take a stand is when students use racist, sexist, or other intolerant language. This is a time to stop the lesson, calmly identify the inappropriate behavior, and remind students of your classroom agreements. It might sound like this: "Just a second, Desiree, but we don't use that language. It's disrespectful and one of our agreements is to respect each other. How else might you express what you're trying to say?"

Not every infraction rises to that level, however. Asking yourself in the moment, "Is this worth confronting?" or "How seriously should I deal with this?" can help deescalate what might otherwise seem like a difficult situation.

I was a first-year teacher trying to get a handle on classroom management. I had a variety of challenges, including a class with some unruly, enthusiastic, and immature eighth-grade boys. I was giving instructions one day when I noticed a lot of commotion in the back of the room. I wasn't very with-it at this point, but it didn't take much skill to realize something was going on back there. These boys were ignoring me and looking at something. I kept teaching my lesson and started walking to the back of the room. As I approached, I saw they were passing something around and giggling. They were oblivious to my presence when I held out my hand to have them give it to me. Embarrassed, they handed me a condom. By now, the whole class was looking at me. I'm sure I turned bright red, but I managed to say, "It's important to have safe sex," smiled at the boys, walked back to the front of the room, put the condom in the trash can, and resumed my lesson.

In our quest to have good classroom management, we often forget that kids are pretty funny and that much of what passes for misbehavior is actually kind of silly. There are few life-or-death situations in the classroom. Keeping a sense of humor and finding places to laugh and smile rather than shout or scowl can be really helpful in building relationships with kids as you're managing the classroom. An arched eyebrow or a wry smile can be just enough of a deterrent to further misbehavior if you have a relationship. A simple "Really?" can sometimes stop inappropriate behavior in its tracks. What the student is doing might actually be worth a chuckle instead of a reprimand.

To be clear, the humor we're talking about never slides into hurtful sarcasm or anything mean spirited or demeaning. The humor should be light, appropriate for the situation, and never cutting or hurtful.

Some Closing Thoughts on Classroom Management

Because students will inevitably misbehave and because you want to work toward their making better choices, avoid *stamp collecting*. This is the idea that teachers collect and hold on to each instance of misbehavior, like a stamp collector keeping their stamps in a book. The student never has a chance to be successful. The student is presumed guilty before they even have a chance to act appropriately. It's not fair. At that point, why should they even try? Instead, approach each day with all your students as a new one regarding their behaviors. A kid may have acted out yesterday but greet them today with a smile and a presumption of innocence. Give each student the benefit of the doubt that they've decided to follow the norms today.

By this point, you might be thinking, "This is all well and good, but I have a class to teach and this takes a lot of time." Yes, it does. But look at the positive outcomes of this approach to classroom management:

- You're taking the time to empower students to help solve classroom management issues, and this helps reduce the number of incidents over time.

- You're modeling solving problems by speaking and listening. There are few other places in the lives of many young people where they can learn and practice this way of dealing with problems.

- You're reinforcing skills and demeanors that are needed to become effective learners, competent adults, and engaged citizens.

- You're devoting time to manage student behaviors using conversation, relationship, listening, and positive attention to make your classroom a humane environment where all students feel accepted and want to learn.

- You're concretely supporting the social and emotional growth of students.

- You're helping everyone in the class find the humor and positive energy in working together productively and with positive intentions.

Where besides your classroom might students find this approach in other parts of their lives? There might be nothing more important than creating a persistently safe environment for learning the skills of collaborative problem solving, conflict resolution, and being in community with others.

Chapter 3

Planning for Engaged and Authentic Learning

As relationships develop, teachers come to know how different students learn and interact in the classroom. Because our classrooms are filled with diverse individuals, our instructional methods must be varied to allow for active, engaged, and authentic learning by all students.

What you'll find in this chapter:

- How to offer students choice in assignments and how they demonstrate their learning

- How to increase each student's ability to be responsible for their own learning

- The importance of differentiating for a diverse student population

- Why authentic and engaging instruction helps motivate students

- Concepts and skills that prepare students to live in a democratic society

- Ideas for creating lessons that engage students in meaning making and wrestling with ambiguity

- Suggestions for crafting authentic and engaging lessons

- How to reduce the amount of content taught so students can explore concepts, topics, and themes in depth

Here's what active and engaged learning looks like:

> Immediately students see that the classroom is arranged like a courtroom today. Five desks are in the front, facing the rest of the students. The remaining desks are set up in two discrete sections facing the five desks in the front. As students gather, the energy is palpable. Today is the mock trial they've prepared for over the previous three days. Student judges take their seats in the front and begin to chat among themselves. They'll be conducting this trial and ruling on the case. The prosecution and defense sit in their groups facing the judges, arranging their notes. The bell rings, and the teacher states that court is in session and defers to the five judges.
>
> The judges call for order, read the charges, and ask for opening statements from the defense and the prosecution. Witnesses are called, examined, and cross-examined. Judges rule on objections and ask their own questions of witnesses, prosecutors, and defense attorneys. Time seems to fly. There is passion in the air as closing arguments are made and the judges adjourn to the hallway. The teacher meets them there and starts a quick debrief of the trial to this point. What were each side's most compelling arguments? What testimony seemed most important? How will they rule and why? She tells them to quickly return to the room when done deliberating. While the judges consider the case, the teacher returns and starts a similar debrief with the class. The judges return to the room and announce their verdict and the reasoning behind their decision. They answer questions about their ruling until the class ends. As kids put away their materials and move to their next class, they argue among themselves about whether the judges made the correct ruling.

An amazing array of content and skills were practiced and learned in this lesson:

- How to speak and listen in public

- How to present and support an argument

- How to use textual evidence

- How to think on your feet

- Knowledge about trial and court procedures

- Knowledge about individual rights

Most students who took this course remember this mock trial activity as one of their favorites. This is an example of active, authentic learning. It demonstrates *students as workers* in the classroom responsible for their learning. They wrestled with ambiguity and engaged in making meaning about what was said and argued in class.

During the trial, the teacher stayed in the background, watching and looking for specific points in the process to focus on in the debrief of the lesson, but they had done a significant amount of planning and preparation beforehand. Students *behaved* because they knew what was expected of them, and they each played a role in the activity. The day of the trial was a culmination of several days of introduction, assigning of roles, and research and preparation in smaller groups. The entire trial was an authentic learning experience—it got students invested in the outcome, and it modeled processes that are part of our judicial system. It was one of those days when it's great to be a teacher!

Choice and Agency in Student Learning

As in the mock trial exercise, teachers want students to care about what they are learning and be positively engaged as often as possible. When relationship is part of the classroom and lessons offer choice in how to demonstrate learning, the potential for energy and enthusiasm is much greater. Students are far more likely to be responsible and motivated. Students with agency are able to act independently and make choices driven by their own interests, and this helps make learning more meaningful and relevant. Greater ownership supports academic achievement. Agency doesn't imply equal power or that the teacher cedes any basic authority structures that are required for them to do their job. It's a sharing of responsibility for how students will go about their learning.

Here are some simple and easy ways to promote agency in the classroom:

- Provide frequent opportunities for students to choose content within the boundaries of the established curriculum.

- Allow varied assessment options for students to demonstrate their learning.

- Trust that students will learn to make appropriate choices when given the opportunity.

You can choose how to direct and encourage students in making these choices. You might suggest a project that is outside a student's comfort zone to challenge them to build skills in an area where they have some weakness. You might offer options that let a student shine, using their strengths to demonstrate their learning.

In a classroom where equity, diversity, and inclusion are valued, offering choice is essential. When you know your students, you can use their culture, ethnic background, gender identity, and experiences to make personal connections to the curriculum. You can give students opportunities to choose materials that portray events and people from diverse perspectives and that represent different voices. This broadening of the curriculum, by including content and voices that are frequently absent in the dominant culture, can be done in just about any content area from language arts to the sciences.

No matter what the demographics of your community or how traditional your curriculum, it is important to broaden the voices and perspectives that your students have access to. Allow students to choose from a wide variety of short stories, poetry, and novels to bring the voices and identities of diverse people into the classroom content. Offering choices can make the curriculum more inclusive by personalizing history or literature or science, which helps build relationship, honor your students' identities, and teach students from majority communities about the voices and experiences of others. These materials help kids see that you and the school really do value all students by making sure the curriculum is diverse. It's an obligation of a culturally responsive teacher and worth the extra effort to find additional teaching materials.

Helping Students Learn to Choose

Choice is important because it helps students learn and practice the responsibilities needed to be a successful worker, partner, lifelong learner, and citizen. Life is filled with the need to make and live with choices.

At first, giving students choice can lead to frustration for the teacher. In the secondary years, many students lack the agency or creativity to make worthwhile choices or even know what interests them at school. When we first gave students the opportunity to make authentic choices about what to study in depth in our courses, we would ask, "What are you really interested in?" and "How do you want to demonstrate what you've learned?" Students would stare at us blankly. They rarely had to make these sorts of choices because school had been a routine of listening to teachers, completing sets of questions or worksheets, and taking tests and quizzes. We would struggle in conversations to find some glimmer of student interest and then try to direct it toward a realistic project of some sort.

A conversation to help a student make a choice might sound like this:

TEACHER: It seems like you can't decide what to focus your project/research/reading choice on.

STUDENT: Yeah, I can't think of anything.

TEACHER: Well, what are you interested in?

STUDENT: I don't know.

TEACHER: No, really, what are some things you like to do? [taking a cue from the skateboarding T-shirt] Do you skateboard?

STUDENT: Yeah, I guess.

TEACHER: What if we think of something that focuses on that?

STUDENT: OK.

TEACHER: Well, since this is science class, do you know what forces in physics influence your movements on the skateboard? Want to know more about that? It might help you with your skills.

or

Well, since this is civics class, do you want to find out how you can change some of the laws around where you can skateboard?

or

Well, since this is literature class, do you want to read a biography of a particular skateboarder and then write about why you think that person is important in the skateboarding world?

or

Well, since this is history class, do you want to research how the sport came into being?

Think about it and let me know if you want some other ideas, OK? I'll check back with you.

It takes time, patience, and a willingness to push past students' learned passivity. Some of them just wanted us to tell them the right answer or what to do to get an A. We felt like we were banging our heads against the wall, but gradually and after a lot of persistence, students began to believe that we cared about what they were interested in and they started to engage. They became more responsible and engaged in their learning. Sometimes we gave a generic assignment and offered choice to those who wanted it. When the students who opted for the basic, generic assignment saw what the students who had made their own choices produced, it inspired them to think about their own possibilities and options. Eventually, students improved at making these sorts of choices and taking a bit of control over their own learning. It was worth the wait and frustration.

It can be relatively easy to give students choice within the confines of any course curriculum. Begin by presenting the basic topic and any necessary background information. Then let students choose how they want to explore it in greater depth and how they want to demonstrate their learning. They can decide if they want to do it through something visual, artistic, narrative, or another way.

Here are some possible activities and tasks that offer student choice:

- Creating an informational brochure or poster combining text, visuals, and layout that goes into depth on one aspect of the lesson content

- Taking a stand in a position paper, persuasive essay, or a letter to the editor

- Writing a fictional historical narrative that demonstrates historical understanding

- Creating a book cover showing understanding of a book and knowledge of the author

- Combining the student's native language and English to create an infographic that teaches the student's community about a topic

- Using technology to present, draw, develop a podcast, or create a website on selected course content

The options are nearly infinite, and it doesn't take much preparation to offer these choices when you have a ready-made list of options for each unit. You can use evaluation rubrics that share common standards related to skills, depth of content presented, and quality of presentation. You can find templates and models for such rubrics online and tailor them to fit your needs. It's also usually more interesting to grade these types of projects.

> In my first year of teaching, I gave a traditional end-of-unit test that had a unit-summarizing essay question. My expectation was that students would write a standard five-paragraph expository essay showing their understanding of the content. Over the weekend, I graded the ninety-five tests from three class sections. The essays were of varying quality, but I stopped short when I saw that instead of an essay one student had written a full-page, free-verse poem that answered the question. I didn't know what to do. The poem addressed all the appropriate content, but the student had ignored my instructions and made a different choice without asking my permission. Pretty brave! The poem was amazing.

It was much better than what many students wrote in their formal essay. It took some time for me to figure out how to evaluate it. Finally, I decided to give the student full credit. They were so proud of what they had written, and I figured I would have many other opportunities to assess their ability to write a formal expository essay. I had just been taught a lesson about choice by a student!

When you give students agency and choice, they will usually be more willing to do what needs to be done when choice isn't an option. They will have more patience while taking tests, practicing writing, or doing math drills because these obligatory tasks are balanced with opportunities to do things of greater interest.

Differentiating Instruction

Differentiation is the personalization of instruction, and it is at the heart of teaching in relationship. Every classroom is filled with a wide variety of students. For example, you may have students who are developing fluency in English or have identified learning challenges and are supported through the special education staff. Some of your neurodivergent students may prefer drawing or speaking to demonstrate their learning. Quite a few students prefer more individualized work. Students who are developing readers and those who love to read all benefit from differentiation, as do developing writers and those who adore writing. A teacher has to take into account students who monopolize discussions and those who won't say a word without being asked. Students who are identified as gifted and talented require differentiation as well as those students who seem to always get good grades but could do so much more if encouraged to go further. Effective teachers have always differentiated their instruction.

As teachers come to better know their students as individuals, they form insights about each student's strengths and challenges. Some students bring a full toolbox of skills to school, while others' toolboxes may be nearly empty. Every student has an equal right to learn and grow in our classroom. A teacher's approach to differentiation says a lot to students about how respect for diversity and relationship really play out in the classroom.

Our attitudes about meeting the diverse needs of students are tied to student success and efforts to close the achievement gap. For example, a culturally responsive teacher views differences in language ability as potential assets in the classroom. Students for whom English is a second language bring their own culture, background, and perspective into the learning environment. This can be encouraged and valued to support relationship and community in the classroom. The thinking that takes place in the student's native language can be brought out into the open when we're all patient. This honors and encourages the student as they do the incredibly difficult job of learning in a new language.

Differentiation means basing instructional decisions on the relationships you develop with students, which starts at the very beginning of the year with greeting them, listening to them, and including them in discussions and activities. This is how you begin to know and address individual strengths and challenges.

Here are some ways to successfully differentiate your instruction:

- Vary your instructional activities (small groups, simulations, lectures, readings, audiovisuals, etc.) and make sure learning is as active and engaged as possible.

- Provide choice for students in the work they do. Allow a variety of options for how they can demonstrate their learning.

- Define expectations and then push all students to improve and meet expectations at increasing levels of rigor. Provide opportunities for revisions of assignments so students learn how to be successful in meeting expectations.

- Find course materials at various reading levels so everyone can successfully access content. Read class materials aloud to those who prefer listening and reading along, regardless of actual language fluency, and allow those who want to read on their own to do so.

- Make time during discussions for students who process at different speeds or are learning in a new language to be able to think before responding. Slow things down!

- Work with students individually and in small groups to coach them in areas where they need growth and improvement.

- Collaborate with English language learners, special education, gifted and talented, and other resource teachers so your efforts in the classroom are supported.

All these approaches will be more possible and more successful when you have positive relationships with your students. They will trust that you have their best interests at heart because you know them well.

Meaningful differentiation also helps students let down built-up defenses and begin to openly engage with teachers and peers as they start to address their unique learning challenges. When a student feels safe in a classroom, they can use a wrong word or get a concept confused without facing ridicule from peers or a dismissive look from the teacher. In a classroom that is safe, risk taking is rewarding instead of anxiety producing.

> James always doodled in class. He seemed unfocused and took few notes when I was presenting content. It annoyed me, so I'd walk over and tap his notebook, indicating that he should pay attention to the lesson. He was a poor writer and didn't do many of the homework assignments. I was working with Kay, a local storyteller who'd received a grant to tell stories about historical events in the local schools. It was a different way to engage students, some of whom I hoped would take to the reenactment of history through story. By the time she came, our class had studied conflicts between whites and Native Americans and about the Holocaust.
>
> Kay came on two successive days. On the first day, she told the story of a young Native American girl who had lived through the Sand Creek Massacre in Colorado in 1864. The next day, she told the story of a girl who survived the Auschwitz-Birkenau concentration camps. The students were clearly moved. I asked them to choose a way to portray what they had learned from listening to Kay's stories. I got essays and creative writing, but the most surprising and powerful was a drawing from James. I wasn't even sure he'd been paying attention. He was visibly proud when he handed me a detailed drawing of how he envisioned the scene of the massacre along Sand Creek, with an image of the crematoria in the concentration camps more faintly in the background. Smoke from chimneys blended with smoke from campfires,

with images of bodies floating into the sky. I was stunned. He really got what Kay was trying to communicate, and he was able to show it in a way that showcased his strengths.

Some students doodle in order to pay more attention to a lesson, much like some people knit while listening to a lecture. It helps unplug a part of their brain so they can concentrate better. This was true for James, and when not hassled about his doodling it gave him more opportunities to show what he knew through art projects. When it was time to focus on writing, James was more willing to engage because he knew he had other options at other times to demonstrate his learning.

Differentiation is about making sure your instruction provides each student with opportunities *to stretch and to shine.* There are few superstars in our classrooms who can do it all—read deeply, write compellingly, draw creatively, think rigorously, and speak powerfully. Plan lessons and assessments that allow for comfort and confidence in what a student is expected to do, as well as times that they can stretch out of their comfort zone. Robust learning requires both.

Authentic Instruction

Authentic instruction motivates students to learn and use concepts and skills in ways that are applicable to life beyond school. It is based around activities that help prepare students for success in future educational pursuits, in the workplace, and in relationships by having them practice skills such as taking initiative, being flexible, and thinking critically.

Here are some authentic learning tasks:

- Organizing a teach-in on a local issue to inform students and others for a civics class

- Creating and publishing a classroom newspaper

- Using geographic information system (GIS) mapping to monitor a local prairie dog population for a biology class or urban waste disposal sites for a geography class

- Doing statistical analyses of public transportation ridership trends for a math class

- Producing an oral history video about an historical event experienced by community or family members for a history class

- Finding nondominant culture narratives and bringing them into the curriculum

- Establishing a system to track and monitor local weather data for a science class

- Using "French fry fractions" where students develop strategies for sizing fractional pieces and develop understanding of the relationship of the size of the numerator and fractional pieces

Worksheets Are Inauthentic

Schools are supposed to prepare students for real life. So why do we often see worksheets in the classroom when worksheets are rarely part of learning in the real world? Worksheets are generally used as tools for compliance—they are easy to grade, and they show parents that their children are busy and have something to do. But worksheets rarely involve using higher-order skills of synthesis, evaluation, and original thinking. They don't provide students with choices or responsibility for their own learning. A worksheet doesn't help a future citizen in a democracy practice the skills needed to be a worker, a partner, or a lifelong learner. Worksheets are at the opposite end of the spectrum from authenticity.

Authenticity from Kindergarten to High School

Think about a kindergartener going off to school for the very first time. For them, school *is* real life. It's counting and imagining and being read to and learning letter shapes and number concepts—all of which are part of becoming a member of the larger community where people use math and read. Kindergarteners cook food and care for classroom animals. These are real-life tasks with authentic purposes. Kids categorize, organize, and build. They learn about money and weather and holidays.

They read age-appropriate books that help socialize them and teach them skills for relationships. A five-year-old can probably tell you why they are in school: something about how they are learning to be a big person. Why isn't all K–12 education as authentic as that?

At some point after kindergarten, the focus on instruction shifts away from real-world tasks. It might happen in first grade, when most children are supposed to learn to read but some haven't yet mastered this basic skill. These students start doing drills and repetitive work, and the joy of reading is replaced by the drudgery of practicing how to do it. Sometime around third grade, mandated testing begins in many districts. Kids come to know that they're being measured, and some don't measure up well. Teaching to the test tends to suck the authenticity out of most learning because students are now learning for the sake of passing the test. Around fourth or fifth grade, we start telling students to do this work to prepare for middle school. That pressure continues in middle school, when teachers feel they need to prepare students for high school. In high school, much of what students hear is focused on getting ready for AP tests or graduation and postsecondary jobs and college.

The notion of *ready for* is devoid of authentic purpose and tends to bend instruction toward disjointed tasks, rote skill development, and coverage of content. The pressure to cover more and more content reduces opportunities for choice, student interest, and purposefulness. Teachers should prepare students to accomplish the authentic demands of real-world adulthood, not the next grade level or the next externally mandated test.

As students mature, they should have more and more opportunities to engage in authentic learning experiences that connect their learning in school with the things they hope to do throughout their lives. Most adults in the real world don't have to sit and listen to lectures or silently complete a repetitive problem set. In the real world, adults as workers and as citizens do an infinite number of authentic tasks from using math for family budgeting to gathering information for a presentation to a boss. We make informed choices during elections and decide how to participate in making the world a better place. Our work requires us to get along with others, problem solve, and come to agreed-upon solutions. We want our classrooms to prepare our students to be involved citizens in a democracy and productive, satisfied workers. The skills associated with all these tasks can be practiced at any grade level while learning social studies, science, math, or any other subject.

Many high school students already work in the real world—as store managers, coders for local startups, or members of landscaping crews. They take on these responsibilities and do great. We can at least give students more responsibility and authentic tasks in the classroom so they can learn and practice the skills they need to become more competent at real-life tasks.

In the not too distant past, individuals often worked the same job for their entire lives. Today, young people expect to change jobs throughout their lifetime. The content of what they do will change, but the skills they need to analyze, make meaning, get along with others, solve problems, and work with diverse colleagues will stay the same. Our responsibility as teachers is to plan and implement lessons that authentically prepare our students for their future.

What is your experience with authentic learning? What did you learn in your K–12 education that gave you skills for your life today? What do you wish you had learned?

From Direct Instruction to Meaning Making

When we make classroom tasks engaging and worthwhile, we don't need to put lectures, textbooks, and worksheets at the core of our instructional methods. The excessive use of these instructional tools is drudgery, pure and simple. And they rarely support the human connections and relationships that we want to see flourish in our classrooms. Most classroom lectures are not like spirited TED talks attended by a paying audience. And playing a video presentation is just another way to provide direct instruction. Even the most exciting lectures relegate students to being primarily passive listeners.

Authentic instruction creates situations where students are engaged in meaning making instead of trying to find answers predetermined by the teacher. Learning to make meaning should be at the very heart of instruction because a central task of life is trying to figure out *what's going on and what am I going to do about it?*

Meaning making doesn't happen when filling out worksheets. A teacher makes meaning when creating a lecture, but it is not what happens when students listen to that lecture, take notes, and regurgitate the information on a test. Meaning making is alive, authentic, ambiguous, thrilling, and frustrating all at the same time. A good, quick check of any instructional plan is to look for the degree to which students will really engage in meaning making.

Using a Pandemic to Create Teaching Activities

Writing this book as the COVID-19 virus spread across the globe made us think about new, authentic, meaning-making teaching activities at the secondary level related to pandemics. Several ideas came to mind.

- In a geography class, use GIS technology and curated websites to track the spread of the disease and its variants from state to state, country to country, and continent to continent. Students could create animations of this movement to better understand the dynamics of a pandemic. Questions to explore might include how transportation plays a role in the relative speed of transmission across regions and to what extent different public policies are successful in limiting the spread of COVID-19.

- In a math class, analyze statistical data on the rates at which COVID-19 spread in various parts of the United States, evaluating different efforts to "flatten the curve" or the impacts of various efforts to lift stay-at-home orders. Students could then figure out how to help the school community understand these complicated data.

- In a history class, examine the similarities and differences in how state, local, and national leaders dealt with the Spanish Flu in 1918–1919 compared with government responses to COVID-19. Students might create a policy handbook for future pandemics. Or compare China's Zero COVID policy with policies in other countries.

- In the sciences, compare the novel coronavirus with other known viruses and developing hypotheses about what made this one so contagious and lethal or compare the uses of the PCR and CRISPR techniques in developing tests and vaccines.

- In a literature class, explore stories and poetry spawned by the pandemic. Students could find these pieces online in blogs and other sources. After reading them, students could write their own stories, poems, or essays.

The Importance of Ambiguity

When authenticity and meaning making drive classroom instruction, teachers have to help students develop comfort with ambiguity. While content is important and is the grist on which the wheels of thinking grind, making sense of ambiguous situations and information is an authentic life skill and important in a democracy. Meaning making is the process by which we do this. Life abounds with ambiguous questions and challenges, from the economic to the political to the personal.

Here are some examples:

- Is that referendum or proposed tax plan on the ballot a good idea?

- Do I believe what I just read on that website? What is a fact and what is an unsupported opinion?

- How much screen time is appropriate for young children?

- At what age should kids be given smartphones?

- What's being done with my personal data, and should I be more vigilant in how I control access to them?

- What are the social and moral implications of the increasingly sophisticated forms of artificial intelligence (AI)?

- How do I, as an individual, address my fears and act to address global climate change?

- Should all citizens be vaccinated?

- What did I learn from this book that would help me be a better person?

- What is the answer to $24 \div 2x (2 + 4)$?

- Should people be able to manipulate DNA to select the genetic characteristics of their children?

- What are the characteristics of a good friend? Am I a good friend?

One of the best ways to make meaning from ambiguous questions is to engage in discussion. In a representative democracy, an essential citizenship skill is the ability to share and communicate ideas with fellow citizens. This is how we learn about the positions and candidates we might support. This is the way (in theory!) that we influence the votes of our neighbors and the legislation passed by our elected bodies. This is what we do with the meanings we make about ambiguous civic and policy questions. Conversation is, truly, the coin of the realm in a democracy. It is through conversation that we address the ambiguous civic questions "What is the common good?" And "How do we attain it together?" The answers to these questions are informed not only by the social studies but by science, math, literature, and the arts. The next chapter explores classroom discussion in much greater detail.

Civic questions related to leadership, policy, and government actions depend on citizens who can work through ambiguity and accept that a different answer might be as valid as their own. Flexibility in thinking, open-mindedness, and the ability to find common ground are extremely important and are frequently lacking in both civil society and our classrooms. Our society may currently suffer from too much ambiguity on the one hand and too little skill for dealing with ambiguity on the other. More and more citizens appear to be throwing up their hands in frustration or anger.

Equally troubling is that democratic discourse and listening to others with respect and an open mind are increasingly rare skills. This is why we have a responsibility to provide students with opportunities to learn about and discuss content that raises ambiguous questions in a safe and constructive environment.

It's also hard for teachers to deal with ambiguity in classrooms. By middle and high school, most students have realized that there are supposedly right and wrong answers to most of the questions posed in classrooms. They tend to believe that their job is to figure out the "right" answer as determined by the teacher and give it back as best they can. In these classrooms, the teacher decides what is correct or incorrect, with few opportunities for student interpretations. Many of our most "successful" students are great at figuring out what the teacher wants and giving it back to them on tests and other assignments. There isn't much room for ambiguity or meaning making in this scenario, and there is no development of the skills needed for well-informed and active engagement in society.

To be clear, when we say instruction should raise ambiguous questions, we aren't talking about alternative facts. Some types of recall questions do have right or wrong answers. But fact-based background information in any discipline is the starting point for dealing with more ambiguous topics and questions. Factual information or content needs to be learned to begin thinking about, reasoning about, and even questioning that content.

For example:

- US history includes a body of information related to the various causes of the Civil War. Teaching with an appreciation for ambiguity uses that information to ask whether the Civil War was inevitable, which causes of the war were more or less important, or what obligations the victorious Union owed to newly freed African Americans or today through reparations. We know that as increasingly diverse voices are brought into the curriculum, some of the once agreed-upon content is challenged. This might take the form of "people's history" and other more inclusive narratives in social studies that add richness to the ambiguity in the lessons. Students can think about how adding different voices might change or deepen an interpretation.

- In literature classes, students can examine and interpret the choices made by characters in short stories and novels with an appreciation for ambiguity. Ambiguity can be enhanced by broadening the diversity of authors that students read so students can appreciate how different cultures and times have viewed choices through different lenses.

- Science, long dominated by white males, is coming to recognize the value of diverse voices and contributions. Exploring how gender or ethnicity might influence the process and methods of scientific discovery and interpretation brings ambiguity into science classes. The entire scientific process is based on getting clarity out of ambiguity.

- Art history is filled with examples of techniques or approaches that are at first ridiculed and later become accepted and valued. This is true from impressionism to abstract modernism to a banana taped to a wall. This is the ambiguity behind the question "What is art?"

Inclusive and culturally responsive teachers bring in diverse voices so students can rethink unquestioned assumptions and allegedly agreed-upon content. Teaching in this way helps prepare students for their lives as adults in a world filled with increasing ambiguity.

> Do you recall a particularly interesting lesson or activity from when you were in school? What made it memorable?

Challenges When Teaching with Ambiguity

One of the hardest challenges for teachers who value wrestling with ambiguity and making meaning with students is that they may feel they do not have the flexibility and skills to be comfortable with the uncertainty they are facing. If there is no single correct interpretation or meaning, how do I evaluate what a student is saying? Should there be some sort of agreed-upon closure to the discussion? Students have the same concerns: What's the right answer? What's going to be on the test, and how will I be graded? Addressing these questions is another part of the detox process for students and teachers.

When the Internet was first gaining use in schools, literature teachers complained that students would rush to the web to find the scholarly interpretations of short stories or novels that had been assigned. Students thought they were successfully gaming the system by coming to class with ready-made interpretations. Skillful teachers began to recognize this and stopped asking questions that could be answered using an Internet search, such as "What are the themes of this short story?" Instead, they ask "Which theme do you think is most compelling, and where do you see this issue in your life or the life you'd like to live?" Students can't find answers to these questions on the Internet, and in answering them, they need to be open to a wide variety of possible responses.

Teachers need to recognize the tension in the classroom between being an expert with the right answers and being one of many participants in an open discussion of ideas. Open discussions require the teacher to practice listening with an open mind to hear multiple responses grounded in the text and supported by clear reasoning instead of a telling students what to know. It's tough and rewarding work and worth a bit of extra anxiety.

When we value ambiguity and meaning making, our role is to help students develop skills to support wrestling with differing ideas. They need to become confident in developing their own ideas instead of depending on our approval of their answers. They need to be able to identify whether a source of information is credible and compare sources as they develop the skills of critical thinking. Students also need to be evaluated on their use of these skills. Criteria and rubrics for evaluating online and other digital resources exist and can be adapted for use in the classroom. Rubrics for assessing critical thinking and reasoning can be modified to fit specific criteria.

Relationship is crucial when exploring ambiguity. We are asking students to put their ideas and concerns out in the public space and be willing to test their ideas. Our classroom needs to be a safe environment for all ideas to be expressed and all voices to be heard. Use the class agreements to ensure this.

When the teacher is culturally inclusive, it's easier for students to embrace ambiguity because the classroom is already open to diversity and divergent thinking. It's exciting and rewarding to hear a powerful insight come from a student who hadn't said much in previous discussions or to hear a reflective "I never thought about it that way."

The teacher who values and teaches with ambiguity also engages in their own critical thinking to ask more open-ended questions and thought-provoking follow-up questions. These push students to go deeper or further in their thinking. It's challenging, it's hard, and it's fun. One reason this is so difficult for most teachers is that during their own schooling, they had few opportunities to participate in these sorts of discussions. Their apprenticeship of observation was filled with lectures and limited, if any, chances to engage in authentic conversation. We will talk about asking good questions in the next chapter.

> Do you think it would be hard for you to teach with an emphasis on ambiguity? Why or why not?

One of our graduates went off to college in New York City, where she enrolled in a seminar course. She was excited because she loved the Socratic seminars that were a central part of her high school experience. The seminar class she enrolled in turned out to be a small class that met weekly with the professor. Students would sit around a large table while the professor held forth on the week's reading, with few opportunities to meaningfully participate. Puzzled at first and then a bit frustrated, she met with the professor during office hours. She explained that at her high school, a seminar was an open-ended conversation about the reading they'd been assigned. The class as a whole worked to make meaning from the text with the help, but not domination, of the teacher. Why, she wondered, wasn't this happening in this class? The professor's response was to say, "Fine, you can lead a discussion about this week's reading, and we'll see how it goes." That week, at the start of class, she explained the basic process of a Socratic seminar to her fellow students and asked an open-ended question from the reading. The discussion was lively and productive, with the professor weighing in but not taking over. This became the pattern for the rest of the semester.

Planning Authentic Activities

One of our greatest pleasures as teachers was figuring out how to use a variety of strategies and activities and still address standards. You can find a nearly limitless array of strategies to help students interact with course content and show their understanding beyond lectures and traditional multiple choice, short-answer, or essay tests. These strategies can help take you off center stage so students will do the important work of thinking and meaning making. These aren't activities for activities' sake. They are practical classroom strategies that help students engage with content and practice lifelong skills. Not all teachers are willing to try this, of course, as Jaye learned.

> I spent the last three years of my career as a high school librarian. Coming from my experience in my classroom, I had a goal of changing students' research in the library to a more authentic, inquiry-based process instead of a cut-and-paste reporting of information. At the start of the school year, a chemistry teacher said she wanted her students to use the library to research an assigned element from the periodic table. I provided the necessary resources but felt that a simple report on an element would be a guaranteed regurgitation of easily copied information.

I suggested having students demonstrate the research on their element in a setting like a social mixer. After completing their research, the students would move around the classroom acting like their specific element to show the teacher that they understood what made their element unique. They would find other elements with which to combine to make real-world gases and compounds. For example, Na would find Cl to form salt, and they would celebrate their connection. Hydrogen would be very popular and would connect with many other elements. So would oxygen. One oxygen would be thrilled to join two hydrogens. Argon would stand passively in the corner ignoring other elements. Everyone could be told to freeze in place and describe their likely interactions with elements nearby.

Sadly, the teacher was beside herself with concerns about the possible chaos of the unscripted performance and how she would assess each student. She could have relied on established classroom agreements to help kids act appropriately in this situation. She could have assessed students by having them create diagrams showing who they interacted with by keeping a log of their interactions. Instead, the teacher decided to have each student hand in a two-page "research" paper.

This vignette took place before the advent of AI platforms. Imagine how it might play out today! By simply typing in a prompt, a credible paper would appear and with a bit of editing get turned in to the teacher. Jaye's idea of the social gathering is somewhat AI-proof. A student has to actually know about their element and its interactions with other elements to successfully complete this assignment. Each interaction is unique and unscripted. These are the sorts of activities that can neutralize the negative impacts of AI in the classroom.

One relatively easy way to plan for ambiguity and bring authenticity into the classroom is to use dilemmas. Dilemmas are authentic and ambiguous questions from history, literature, or science. The dilemma itself can provide the basic content, or the teacher can present the dilemma after students have learned some background content. The lesson focuses on how to resolve the dilemma: Should President Polk have asked Congress to declare war on Mexico in 1846? Should the main character in the book *No-No Boy* sign a loyalty oath to get out of a Japanese American internment camp? Should we allow genetic manipulation of a human embryo for traits like height or athletic skills? Should a police department use facial recognition technology despite evidence of embedded racial bias? These are questions that students love to learn more about and discuss. There is no need for the class to agree on a conclusion; each student can have an opportunity in a position paper, podcast, or other format to state and defend their own position.

Dilemmas are not limited to the domain of social studies. Science classrooms are places where students can learn not only about biological or chemical processes but also about how to interpret and make sense of bioethical questions or how chemicals affect our daily lives. Literature raises eternal questions of right and wrong, good and evil, moral and immoral. Classrooms might be the only place where students have opportunities to engage with these sorts of discussion topics. We'll say more about this in chapter 4 when we explore the teaching of controversial issues.

Classroom management issues diminish as students engage with compelling and authentic discussions. It does take practice becoming comfortable managing these types of discussions and dealing with the wide-ranging back and forth that often takes place. If you are new to this or are a new teacher, try it first in short lessons where you begin by just raising the pros and cons of the question. Use the classroom agreements and your practice with small groups to support these discussions and extend them. Troubleshoot with a colleague to resolve problems you might encounter. You will enjoy the results of your efforts as you witness the energy and attention students bring to making sense of your interesting lessons.

Engaging Instructional Activities to Try

- Simulations
- Role plays
- Meeting of the Minds
- Debates
- Scored Discussions
- Card sorts
- Rank orders
- Jigsaws
- Carousel brainstorming
- Socratic seminars

- Poster projects
- Research projects
- Experiments
- Opinion continuum
- Speed dating
- Concept maps
- Creative writing
- Brochures
- Case studies
- Structured Academic Controversy

Protest and Reform in US History was a popular unit at the school. Students studied various historical events through the lens of protest and reform using a variety of activities. They learned content related to the American Revolution, abolition, and the civil rights movement, as well as methods for bringing about social and political change. The final project for this unit was to identify a problem in the school or local community and then engage to fix it.

When students asked if they could fire the principal, the answer was no. Instead, they were encouraged to work with teacher groups and parents to identify problems in the school that could realistically be addressed. Part of the learning was discovering the limits and boundaries of protests. Students learned where to focus their energy, how to identify obstacles, and how to find resources to overcome them.

Students worked hard on these projects because it was their problem, and they were invested in bringing about change. Not all the actions were successful, but the engagement and learning were significant. Some students even continued working on their project after the unit ended. One group eventually convinced the local municipality to install a safer crosswalk near the school by writing letters and lobbying local officials. Another group succeeded in getting the administration to change the school's lunch schedule to better meet student needs.

The authenticity of this final project drove student interest and engagement because the topics were of real concern and were identified by the students, not the teacher. It is also a good example of how classroom learning can support the democratic purposes of schools. Students were listened to as credible spokespersons for their cause because they had developed deep knowledge about the problem they were hoping to resolve. They were able to present solid arguments for change and support them with research and evidence. They were passionate about accomplishing their goals. For what it's worth, one of those students was elected to the local city council several years later after returning to the community and setting up a business.

In this unit, the teacher directed the activities in the classroom instead of being the central repository of course content. There were times of direct instruction as well as large- and small-group activities. When working on the final project, students sought counsel from the teacher on next steps, how to overcome obstacles, and how to find local experts and other resources. The teacher went from small group to small group as assistance was needed and to ensure that students were on task. The teacher acted as a consultant as ideas were generated and when students wanted feedback on their writing. At other times, there was little for the teacher to do because the students were highly engaged in the work.

We can't lie—not every lesson or every unit has this degree of authenticity and engagement, nor can every lesson be this authentic. But developing a collection of engaging lessons is a good start. You can keep adding to it year after year.

> A colleague who taught a creative writing class had her secondary students work with first graders to write a personalized storybook for them. Each of her students interviewed a younger kid to find out their interests and then created an illustrated storybook specifically for their first-grade partner. This project involved learning about writing children's literature and then interpersonal skill development, listening, creativity, diligence in writing the actual story, and attention to quality in crafting the final product.

Degrees of authenticity are found in activities such as this. We say degrees of authenticity because it's very hard within the structures of nearly all schools to find consistent opportunities for real authenticity. The challenge for teachers is to move our instructional activities toward a goal of more and more authenticity so that what students do in classrooms increasingly reflects the tasks and skills required outside of the school environment.

Technology can help us create more flexible instruction with innovative ways to support active and engaged learning. A first step is to make sure all students have equal access to the Internet and related technologies. Technology can then broaden agency and choice and make it easier to engage in authentic activities outside the classroom, school, and community such as in the following examples:

- Accessing a wider range of verifiable, fact-based information helps students learn appropriate research and text evaluation skills

- Video conferencing with experts can help bring the real world into the classroom.

- Podcasts, blogs, and websites are sources that citizens regularly use to access information, express ideas, and see democracy in action.

- Cartooning, digital stories, digital art, and photography are exciting ways for students to use technology to create and share their work.

- Software technology for videos, slideshows, slow-motion animation, and digital presentations supports project-based learning.

- Collaboration software allows students to engage with a far wider range of other young people in communities different from their own.

- Online, threaded discussions help students think about and begin articulating ideas to jump-start larger discussions and the meaning-making process. They also provide important skills for the real world of jobs and communication.

ChatGPT and other AI programs have entered into our daily lives. Among the first to panic were teachers. Would this be the end of assigning essays for students to write? Would homework disappear because it could be done by asking an AI program to complete it? Would there now be an arms race between cheaters and the systems to identify and defeat the cheaters?

Teachers are figuring out ways to use AI in the pursuit of engaging instruction.

- Students could use AI to help develop outlines for an essay. Based on these outlines, each student then writes their own complete essay during class. Here, AI is used to scaffold the essay writing, with students responsible for the final essays that are written without use of AI.

- The class can work individually, in small groups, and as a whole class to brainstorm topics and outlines for essays or text-based projects. AI programs can then be used to write essays or text based on this work. Students are then responsible for critiquing the AI-generated essays and text and improving them.

- AI can help prepare students for discussions. Once in discussions, students have to express and explain their ideas as they inquire into the content without the assistance of the AI program.

- AI can help teachers create lessons plans, generate questions and prompts for discussions, and even assist in evaluating student work.

Like other new and powerful technologies, creative teachers committed to authentic instruction can find ways to use and leverage technology instead of being constrained by it. What AI can't do is replace the important relationships you're building with your students. These relationships help you and your students navigate many of the issues AI is likely to present.

Interactive presentation tools, video clips, graphics, and other audiovisual elements are ways to keep students actively engaged in lessons, as well as a means to keep your lessons fresh. While all this is exciting, low-tech instructional strategies still have a place in your teaching repertoire.

We often found inspiration for, and examples of, active and engaged instructional activities at state and regional teacher conferences. Early in our career, several curriculum development centers received federal funds to create and disseminate excellent teaching materials that had the qualities of authenticity and rich meaning making. Many of those materials still exist online and there are still centers in most content areas that are producing new and exciting curriculum materials. Universities have associations or institutes that generate curriculum on foreign policy, geography, specific countries, history, US and world literature, math, and science. Professional organizations for different subject areas produce excellent, content-based instructional activities. Working with colleagues to conceive and implement engaging lessons is also a great way to move toward more authenticity. We'll say more about this in chapter 6.

What is one lesson or unit that you could make more authentic and engaging?

Flipping Your Classroom to Increase Engagement

Classroom time is precious when teachers create engaging lessons that require meaning making and wrestling with ambiguity. It takes time to think and discuss and make meaning. One method that has given teachers more time to go in depth and run interactive activities is the use of the flipped classroom.

Teachers who flip their classrooms have students access lectures, readings, or other information outside of class, usually as homework, and then use class time for meaning-making activities such as discussions and many of the activities we recommend in this book. Flipped classrooms can support relationship, personalization, and authentic engagement. When students are in class, the teacher has more flexibility to work one on one with those who need help completing the assignment associated with the online presentation, whether they are second language learners, special education students, or regular education students. And all students work to make sense of the content with the help of the teacher, in real time. Advanced students can explore additional content independently. This contrasts with more traditional homework, where students are often expected to come to their own understandings at home, which can be a struggle for some.

The best-case use of flipped instruction is to have more time for class discussions, meaning making, and understanding instead of having students passively listen to content being delivered, but a flipped classroom can also be the worst form of instruction. Listening to a lecture online or doing a reading the night before only to come to class and passively complete worksheets defeats the purpose of flipping instruction. New models of technology-based instruction don't serve student learning if the technology is used to do the same old drill and kill in service of covering content. YouTube videos can be as boring as the filmstrips and movies available in times past. Passively watching an online documentary is no substitute for an activity that lets students wrestle with disparate information and piece together their own narrative. Keeping relationship, human connection, and the value of authentic, engaging activities at the forefront can help you critique new technologies and twenty-first-century approaches to learning.

One other caution is not to overdo flipping the classroom. As we talk about in chapter 5, we need to be judicious in the amount of homework and outside of class work we assign. Students have busy lives and have needs for downtime. Part of building relationships with students is respecting the complicated lives of teens.

Teachers should be sensitive to their students' access to technology outside of school. The COVID-19 pandemic highlighted the inequity of access to technology by students, teachers, and families. Not all families or communities have high-speed Internet, access to platforms, and up-to-date hardware. This existed before the pandemic and will remain a challenge into the foreseeable future. Other issues of equity exist for families that cannot afford the latest computers, phones, AI programs, and tools like 3D printers. Some students have no place at home where they can safely or quietly access technology and many families do not have the skills to use technology effectively. Schools and teachers must address these situations that lead to inequities in the work students can produce or content they can access. Teachers should make sure when they assign homework, flipped classroom or not, that students have access to the Internet and computers that can run necessary software. And teachers should not forget that students should be taught the skills to use technology before they are expected to use it by themselves.

The Tension between Depth and Coverage

If you want students to engage with content in discussions and interactive activities, you have to omit some of the material you are expected to teach. In the Protest and Reform in US History unit we described earlier, students explored only a few protest movements to understand the concepts and the historical contexts of protest and reform. If you really want students to have the opportunity to develop the skills of thinking, speaking, listening, writing, and reasoning, you have to leave out some content. There is no way you can adequately cover all that material if students are authentically learning and demonstrating knowledge and skills. We encourage you to go in depth on content you have curated and deemed important enough to include in your curriculum. It's not easy, but it can be done.

Most teachers are expected to teach using curriculum guides packed with too many facts, concepts, themes, and more. These guides provide a suggested scope and sequence for nearly every grade level and content area. There have been efforts in recent decades to reduce the amount of content teachers are expected to teach. The original intent of the standards movement in the 1980s and 1990s was to define a more limited set of critical information and skills that students needed to learn in school and to define better ways to assess that learning. Unfortunately, these efforts were generally unsuccessful because various stakeholders—particularly content experts and advocates in the political sphere—made it impossible to prune the curriculum. Subsequent work on the Common Core State Standards and the 21st Century Skills was built around proficiencies rather than endless lists of names, dates, and facts. Because of the COVID-19 pandemic we are seeing new ideas and changes to how we address standards. Regardless of national and state standards, instruction that explores topics in depth and develops the skills of thinking, speaking, listening, writing, and reasoning can coexist with whatever your state requires.

Here's an example of an in-depth lesson a colleague developed in a unit on the concept of civilization for a world history class.

> The focus of the lesson is Chaco Canyon, an important civilization in the southwest of what is now the United States. It flourished for several hundred years and then was mysteriously abandoned about one thousand years ago. The lesson begins by brainstorming the characteristics of a great civilization to engage students and activate their prior knowledge. The list gets whittled down to an agreed-upon set of proposed characteristics. Two questions are posed: What happened at Chaco Canyon? And is Chaco Canyon representative of a "great" civilization? There are two days of in-depth study of the culture at Chaco Canyon. Students look at slides of archeological sites, review data on rainfall and patterns of interaction with other peoples in the area, and more. The raw data are from online sources and a National Geographic magazine.
>
> The students examine the data in small groups and then begin trying to figure out why Chaco Canyon, once a thriving culture, was suddenly abandoned. It's an authentic question because archeologists still don't agree on the answer. Students know that they are each expected to propose and defend their own hypothesis. Next, students explore the question of whether Chaco Canyon was a great civilization. A lively discussion ensues, with students required to apply the class's criteria for a great civilization. The same criteria are used to evaluate other civilizations as the course progresses.

Students make passionate arguments in favor of different interpretations of the data. Some raise questions linking climate issues that the people of Chaco Canyon faced with current concerns about the impacts of global climate change. Students apply the criteria to the question of whether the United States represents a great civilization.

Assessment of this lesson isn't difficult. Students compile information and evidence on data collection forms. These are checked off when complete. As students work in small groups, the teacher takes notes that will inform each student's class participation grade. After the large-group discussions about the essential questions, students have the option of writing a position paper explaining their interpretation, recording a podcast on the essential questions, or making a fictional visitor's guide to Chaco Canyon outlining the important aspects of the mystery and their theory of what happened. A standard rubric guides evaluation of the students' work.

After this lesson, instead of having the students study civilization after civilization as a whole class, the teacher had each student choose from a menu of civilizations over the span of world history to examine on their own. The students presented what they learned in a "celebration of world history" gallery walk where they learned from one another. This was far more engaging and allowed for individual interest and motivation. Students ended the unit by writing a personal essay explaining which of the civilizations they would choose to live in and linking their choice to what they believed were the most important characteristics of a civilization.

The choice of Chaco Canyon, a culture usually not studied in depth in world history classes, for the initial lesson also reinforced diversity goals by broadening the content beyond the standard course curriculum. A similar activity might focus on the culture of Great Zimbabwe in southern Africa.

Dealing with Too Much Content

How rebellious should a teacher be in resisting the pressures of the curriculum guidelines and school administrators to cover the required curriculum or teach to the test? A balance must be struck. We believe that a bit of thoughtful subversion is called for in this situation. By being subversive we mean (especially as a beginning teacher) striving to design units where you ditch some of the content and focus on larger themes or more authentic inquiry questions. On the other hand, listen to the voices of your administrators and the community to know when it might be unwise to step outside of the prescribed boundaries. You need to pick your battles, and this might not be the time to risk your job. If this is the case, make whatever subtle changes you can while still meeting the expectations of your administration and the school district.

Here are some ways to prune and ditch content:

- Use your own content knowledge to identify what you think is relatively more important to keep or toss.

- Use your passion to choose content that you are excited to teach.

- Join with a colleague or a curriculum coach and discuss what content or units might work best for understanding a standard, concept, theme, or time period and what might be OK to prune.

- Identify and select topics in your content area that are most likely to help students make connections to their own lives and prepare them for the future. (Chaco Canyon was a great way to connect history to current issues related to global climate change.)

- Find resources online or from workshops that can help guide you as you make decisions about what to teach and what to eliminate.

Pruning the curriculum and developing these types of activities is a gradual process that takes practice. With patience, you will amass a collection of both generic and specific activities for lessons and units over time.

To support your efforts to be safely subversive and teach topics in depth, document your work. Collect evidence demonstrating that this approach leads to student learning and achievement. As you teach these units, look at your student assessments and analyze what they reveal. Did students successfully demonstrate their learning about the topic and the skills they used? Do you see any gaps in understanding or areas where more background knowledge was needed? Survey your students and see what they thought about the work you assigned and what they think they learned and are now able to do. If you are worried about your evaluation or your administrator not supporting you, set up a meeting with them to explain and demonstrate the results you are getting as you teach with more depth and less coverage. Have student vignettes ready that show how a variety of learners did in this teaching approach. Invite administrators in to observe your terrific lessons!

We got rid of survey courses at New Vista so we could focus on depth instead of coverage. We found that the skills and content we taught in depth were transferable, as evidenced by student success on state and district assessments and later in college. We taught students to think by using rich content in our courses. When taking mandated assessments, students had the problem-solving and thinking skills to do just fine. Our scores were in line with other schools in the district that had more conventional course offerings. The same was true for our students' college experiences; they arrived with strong thinking, reasoning, and speaking skills that they could use to engage with new content.

Teaching in Depth

Another way to decide what is more or less important to teach is to determine which broad concepts can be applied to a variety of topics, as illustrated in the Chaco Canyon lesson. In secondary history classes, we study wars of independence and national and world wars in the eighteenth and nineteenth centuries, usually one war after another. All wars have common elements, such as the causes of the conflict, the motivations of the contesting parties, who won and how, and the outcomes and consequences of the conflict. If you try to study every war, there isn't time to delve into other aspects of war such as peace efforts or the role of women or people of color. There isn't time to study wars that might interest international students, students of color, or Native American students.

To be more inclusive and look at fewer wars in depth, you might have the whole class study one war and then have students choose a conflict that interests them to explore on their own or in a small group. You can have them apply relevant criteria and concepts from the war that the whole class studied together.

The following examples are from ninth- and tenth-grade Common Core State Standards from English language arts that match a unit on war. Your state and local standards would probably work as well. Students who use primary and secondary resources for their work can demonstrate their proficiency in many of these areas.

CCSS.ELA-Literacy.RH.9-10.1

Cite specific textual evidence to support analysis of primary and secondary sources, attending to such features as the date and origin of the information.

CCSS.ELA-Literacy.RH.9-10.2

Determine the central ideas or information of a primary or secondary source; provide an accurate summary of how key events or ideas develop over the course of the text.

CCSS.ELA-Literacy.RH.9-10.3

Analyze in detail a series of events described in a text; determine whether earlier events caused later ones or simply preceded them.

CCSS.ELA-Literacy.W.9-10.1

Write arguments to support claims in an analysis of substantive topics or texts, using valid reasoning and relevant and sufficient evidence.

CCSS.ELA-Literacy.W.9-10.2

Write informative/explanatory texts to examine and convey complex ideas, concepts, and information clearly and accurately through the effective selection, organization, and analysis of content.

Not so long ago, students in US history classes were required to memorize the names of US presidents. Of what value is the list of names or that assignment? On the other hand, thinking about the qualities of what makes a good or effective president without ever testing those qualities against the actions of actual presidents would be hollow. A meaningful instructional activity using this content might involve generating a list of desired presidential qualities and then working with a partner or a small group to apply those qualities to specific presidents in US history to evaluate or compare their presidencies. Another activity might involve having groups of students run mock presidential campaigns in which different presidents run against each other or run a Meeting of the Minds, with each student playing the part of a different president.

Here are more examples of teaching in depth and demonstrating learning in meaningful ways that are supported by state or district standards:

- Learn about specific chemical compounds, and structure a mock EPA hearing on whether or how those compounds should be limited in the environment.

- Use Bacon's Rebellion as a way to bring counternarratives into the study of settler colonialism and racism.

- Introduce imperialism as a concept and explore it through a case study. Then have students research it in greater depth by focusing on a particular example of imperialism.

- Explore an agreed-upon literary analysis model for one writer from a specific time period including an examination of significant historical influences. Have each student choose their own writer to research from that time period, and during a fishbowl activity (where an inner circle discusses while an outer circle observes) have them share how their writer is a product of the historical period. Ask how they fit or don't fit the literary analysis model for the first writer.

- Learn about the branches of government and federalism and then have students figure out how to get a special part of their state designated as a national monument or historic site.

- Study the geography of Africa in small groups and then have students figure out a proposed route for a pan-Africa highway and vote on the best option based on a predetermined set of criteria.

- Study the life cycle of butterflies using literature, myths, and art. Get caterpillars and watch them turn into butterflies.

Other dynamics can arise when you are open to planning in this way. First, it can be easier to incorporate student choice in your planning.

In the example above, the unit on wars of the twentieth century might begin with a case study that you identify and structure. A student who is more interested in contemporary issues can study current conflicts, while the history buff can go back in time. Other students might want to explore diverse voices and war experiences not usually covered in traditional textbooks or histories.

We're not advocating going totally rogue in your teaching responsibilities. Rather, we are supporting the hard and important choices every teacher must make in planning for courses, units, and lessons. Take a careful look at your curriculum and decide to go deep where it makes the most sense. Eliminate areas of coverage where you can. If your teaching situation is such that making any change to your curriculum is impossible, you can still teach creatively and have great relationships with your students if you are committed to knowing them and treating them with respect. Teaching for depth is important, but so is keeping your job!

Chapter 4

Teaching with Discussion

Discussion is at the heart of what citizens do in a democratic society. Discussion in small and large groups should be a central skill of every teacher's pedagogy. Using discussion in your class promotes learning, helps engage students, and reinforces classroom agreements. Discussions are also where students learn to work with controversial topics that they are likely to face as citizens.

What you'll find in this chapter:

- Why discussion is so important for active and engaged learning

- How to distinguish student talk from discussion

- Ways to structure class discussions

- Suggestions for planning good questions to ask in discussions

- How to practice discussion skills so students improve participation over time

- How to address student discomfort with and participation in discussions

- Tips and suggestions for how to improve large- and small-group discussions

- Reasons to include controversial issues in your curriculum and how to teach about them more confidently

Meaning Is Made in Discussions

Discussions are among the most important ways that students actively engage in and learn course content. In worthwhile discussions, students explore possible meanings, offer tentative interpretations, and introduce new ideas or evidence. They participate in a back-and-forth conversation of ideas as they consider interpretations using the facts and concepts they're learning. They use listening and analytical skills to evaluate the validity of differing interpretations. The ambiguity that is often at the center of interesting classroom discussions means students see multiple meanings instead of a single right answer that receives the teacher's stamp of approval.

The reward for the teacher is that students are doing intellectual work rather than passively listening to and writing down your answers. Students will amaze you with their insights and interpretations when you allow them the structure and space to do so.

Recall, for a moment, the mock trial and the lesson on Chaco Canyon. Both activities involved rich content and gave students opportunities to actively engage with that content. In the trial, the attorneys had to discuss which arguments would be persuasive. The judges had to discuss how they would rule and why. Small and large groups discussed why Chaco Canyon was abandoned and whether it met the criteria for a great civilization.

When students participate in discussions, they have opportunities to learn and practice a wide range of discrete skills that, together, help them competently speak, listen, think, and reason. They include:

- Expressing opinions, taking positions, and supporting them with evidence

- Making and evaluating claims

- Paraphrasing, asking questions, and linking ideas

- Listening to hear and understand what other people are trying to say and building on ideas

- Listening with an open mind rather than waiting to argue a personal viewpoint

- Working collaboratively to understand and/or solve a problem

- Disagreeing respectfully, expressing and acknowledging emotions, and showing concern for others in the discussion

- Thinking creatively and flexibly and improving oral language skills

These skills empower the diversity of learners in our classrooms to participate in school, society, and our democracy more successfully. They can all be found, similarly worded, in various state and national standards, the WIDA Standards and lists of 21st Century Skills.

We know rigorous discussions are rare in classrooms and that thoughtful dialogue is a diminishing characteristic of our social and civil discourse. Your classroom can be where students learn and practice discussion skills while working together to make meaning.

Why Don't Teachers Use Discussion More?

Teachers avoid conducting classroom discussions for a variety of reasons. Perhaps at the top of the list is the concern that there just isn't enough time to bring student voice and discussion into the classroom. There's already too much content to cover and student talk/discussions are seen as inefficient ways to cover material. Teachers might not have confidence in their own abilities to lead or structure discussions, which matches a concern that students don't have the skills to engage in quality discussions. Some teachers avoid asking for student voice because they fear a loss of control over the content, that students might somehow say something inappropriate or bring in controversial topics. Many teachers are wary of bringing the contemporary culture wars into their classrooms. Teachers are uncertain about how to grade or evaluate discussions and student talk. As you know by this point, we believe that all these concerns can be readily addressed in a classroom that is oriented around relationships, inclusion, and authentic learning.

Discussions do take time, but efficiency isn't the goal of active and engaged instruction. Going deep requires creating opportunities to use, reflect on, manipulate, and interact with content. In discussions, student misconceptions or misunderstandings are often revealed as they explain and grapple with ideas and concepts. Providing for regular and consistent discussions is well worth the expenditure of precious instructional time as you balance the tension between coverage and depth.

> Reflect on these teacher concerns about discussion or others you might have. What excites and worries you about student talk and discussion in your classroom?

Distinguishing between Discussion and Student Talk

We value student talk because it engages students and helps them take ownership of their learning. There are many, many ways in which students might talk in our classrooms such as answering questions, talking with partners, sharing, describing, debating, and reporting out from small groups. Students who have been marginalized or silenced can gain a sense of efficacy and empowerment in classrooms by talking. Student talk can be used as a type of formative assessment, and it can help build a learning community.

There are also potential challenges associated with student talk including a possible loss of control over what's going on in a lesson, managing unequal participation, and students making unhelpful comments. On balance, student talk has far more benefits than drawbacks and we need to do all we can to bring our students' voices into our classrooms and lessons.

While we value student talk in general, it is important to distinguish it from what we mean when we talk about discussion. Discussion is a particular form of student talk that needs to be carefully structured and practiced. Discussion is characterized by two critical elements: inquiry and meaning making. When students are engaged in discussions, they are working to understand the topic at hand. They are inquiring together as they come to both common and personal understandings of the focus of the discussion. This is distinguished from other forms of student talk that involve sharing, describing, and reporting out.

For students to become better at participating in discussions, they need to practice using all sorts of student talk. Each opportunity to share with a partner or report out after a small-group activity or turn and talk during a lecture helps build confidence and skills that are crucial for participating effectively in discussions. In this chapter, we focus on improving discussion in your classroom, but you'll see lots of suggestions and strategies that are more general forms of student talk. All of these have roles to play in your pedagogy.

Student Talk and Discussion Formats: Large and Small Groups

Discussion can take place in a variety of settings and be built around various types of instructional activities. The most basic distinction is between large- and small-group discussions. Large-group discussions allow the entire class to interact with course content and make meaning from instructional activities with the facilitation of the teacher. These discussions are usually based on a combination of questions that check for understanding and more open-ended questions that encourage students to inquire about the topics at hand. Large-group discussions also have their challenges.

Small-group discussions provide opportunities for more students to have voice at the same time. When seven or eight small groups are working at the same time, more students have opportunities to participate instead of one voice at a time in a whole-class discussion. Because of the smaller size, some students are more comfortable participating. These discussions usually begin with a prompt or a question from the teacher and are guided by a handout that lists discussion questions and how students will show accountability for their work.

Some structures for organizing student talk and discussion are better suited to some situations than others and each has different variations and ways of being implemented. As you review the table below, think about which structures are more likely to generate student talk and which more likely to generate the inquiry and meaning making that are needed for discussion to take place. Our job is to be familiar with a wide range of formats so we can choose an appropriate one for a particular learning outcome or topic.

Table 4.1. Student talk and discussion structures

Structure	Description	Comments
Fishbowl	An inner circle discusses while an outer circle observes. You can switch them partway through or leave empty seats for individuals to move in and out of the circles.	• Helps keep discussion groups smaller, but the teacher remains the facilitator • Leads to high-interest listening when each small group is given a different topic • Students practice listening skills when in the outer circle
Socratic seminar	A whole-class, text-based discussion that begins with an opening question and leads to a deeper understanding of the text.	• A powerful way to engage students in meaning making • No agreed-upon answer and no planned outcome of the discussion • Emphasizes practicing discussion skills
Think/Pair/Share	Individual students are asked to think and write down ideas, then they share with a partner, and then the conversation moves to the larger group.	• Gets all kids talking at the start • Can help jump-start a discussion but is often centered on sharing • Especially useful for ELL students
Turn and Talk	After presenting information, the teacher asks a question and tells students to turn to their neighbor to share thoughts and ideas.	• A good way to break up direct instruction • Helps students make meaning in smaller pieces and with a partner during lectures • A safe way for all students to share thoughts and opinions

Structure	Description	Comments
Last Word	A formal structure where after an assignment or conversation, each student has an opportunity to share a final thought or insight.	• A safe way for each student to summarize and have the floor to share ideas • Highly structured
Structured Academic Controversy (SAC)	A specific process for learning about and discussing controversial issues that starts with pairs, then moves to quads, and then moves to the larger group.	• A way to teach controversial issues with a very clear structure • Examples can be found online and elsewhere
Speed dating	Students get in two lines that face each other. The teacher asks a question or gives a topic. The students facing each other have a minute to share thoughts and ideas. Then one line shifts down so everyone has a new partner, and the process repeats.	• An effective way to have all students start talking and thinking in a safe situation • Helps build community to make students more comfortable sharing thoughts and ideas • Gives students a chance to get out of their seats
Gallery walk	Student work or information of some sort is posted around the room. Small groups of students walk around together to view/read the posted material and talk about it. The groups shift stations sequentially until they have stopped at all of them.	• A different way of sharing student work • Reinforces small-group discussion skills • Gives students a chance to get out of their seats

continued on next page

Table 4.1. Continued.

Structure	Description	Comments
Hot seat	One student is the focus of questions in either a large- or small-group setting. They might take on the role of a historical character, a character in a novel, or even something like a water molecule.	• Allows for deeper exploration because the focus is on the thoughts and ideas of one student at a time • Allows other student to practice question-asking and listening skills
1-2-4/Snowball/ mono-dyad-quad	Students first write down a response to a prompt. Then they compare responses with a partner and come to a common and shared response. The process is repeated in a foursome, which again has to come to an agreed-upon response. Finally, the students share their quad's response in a large-group discussion.	• Builds ideas and discussions gradually, from the individual to larger groups • Allows students to work together to support one another's ideas as the group size increases • Values listening and coming to shared understandings
Go-around share	The teacher asks a question and then goes around the room getting a brief reply from every student. General discussion can proceed from there or it can end after the sharing.	• A structured way to hear from every voice at the start of a large- or small-group discussion • Helps increase likelihood of future contributions
Forced choice	The teacher reads a statement to the class, and students have to either agree or disagree with it. Discussion proceeds in large or small groups.	• Allows discussion to flow naturally as students explain, defend, and think about their decisions

Structure	Description	Comments
Opinion continuum	The teacher reads a thought-provoking statement. Students are directed to get up and place themselves along a continuum at the front of the room, with "strongly agree" on one end and "strongly disagree" on the other. Students then share why they are standing at their particular location and compare their choice to others along the continuum. The emphasis is on calibrating one's opinion/location relative to other students.	• As with forced choice, gives students something to talk about • Requires students to speak, listen, and keep an open mind as they calibrate their position along the continuum • Allows students to change their minds and move to a different part of the continuum • Students who are uncertain can be in the middle and make up their mind after hearing all the viewpoints
Corners	The same as forced choice, but students have four choices and go to the corner that best represents their position on the question. Discussion at the corners is followed by a whole-class discussion about the different positions.	• Allows discussion to flow naturally within and between groups • Allows students to move to a different corner if they are influenced by the discussion

continued on next page

Structure	Description	Comments
Online structures	These might be threaded, synchronous, asynchronous, or in the form of a chat or other structure. Each online format requires students to weigh in on teacher-generated questions and/or questions and comments from fellow students.	• Students have different comfort levels with online formats for sharing thoughts and ideas • Typing can be safer and more comfortable for some students than speaking • Need to address issues of equity in access to technology

More details on how to effectively use these structures and their variants can be found in teacher resource materials, online, and from colleagues. Nearly all our suggestions for facilitating face-to-face discussions are also useful when teaching online.

Online and Virtual Discussions

The shift in the spring of 2020 to nearly universal online instruction due to the COVID-19 pandemic was dramatic. After that swift pivot, teachers gained experience facilitating student discussions online using a wide variety of platforms. What they learned is that student voice and discussion are as important online as in face-to-face instruction—maybe even more important in some ways because of the relative isolation students experienced when learning from home. Discussion encourages connections among students and continues to be a powerful way to promote thinking, reasoning, speaking, and listening.

It isn't any easier to conduct discussions and promote student voice online, but it isn't necessarily much more difficult. Students still need to know that their teacher and fellow students value their contributions and will listen to what is said with an open mind and respect. Ideas still need to be grounded in content, and teachers have to be open to new and creative interpretations that might go beyond expected answers. Some students will still be more reluctant to participate, and some will participate too much or too insistently. Some students who struggled with live conversations thrive in an online discussion forum.

Seeking student voice and conducting discussions is different in a virtual setting. Not all online platforms, for example, show the screen of every student, which means you don't necessarily know who wants to contribute except through things like the hand raise function. It is also harder to read body language and nonverbal cues in general. Wait time is different because the students and the teacher can't readily sense who might be willing to make a comment. Some students find it difficult to have the camera on because of where they are located, so they show up as an icon of some sort or just their name. When a student chooses to turn their camera off that must be addressed. These factors may present obstacles to bringing student voice and discussions into your online instruction, but they are not insurmountable.

Most online platforms have a hand raise function that can alert you and others that someone wants to contribute. You can use the participant list to facilitate a go-around share. Students can put ideas into the chat when directed by you to do so as a lower-anxiety way of sharing ideas. Random grouping functions can put students into small groups more quickly than by moving desks around and can bring them back to the large group quickly. Activities like Think/Pair/Share and Turn and Talk can be conducted in the same way as in face-to-face classrooms.

Monitoring small groups can be a bit more of a challenge online, however. In a face-to-face classroom, the teacher can easily wander around the room, listen in on small-group conversations, and keep students on task. Online, the teacher can drop into small groups only one at a time. This means that instructions for small groups must be extremely clear and available in chat for students to reference and use. Assigning of small-group roles such as timekeeper, facilitator, and recorder/reporter is more important to make sure that each group stays on task and on time. Reporting out from discussions is also a bit more challenging. Whiteboards, shared docs, the shared chat, and other tools can facilitate gathering ideas from small-group discussions and support accountability for small-group work.

Virtual Threaded Discussions

Virtual threaded discussions on a variety of learning management systems are usually initiated by a prompt from the teacher, with students typing their responses to the opening question and then to the contributions of their fellow students. Such conversations can have many of the characteristics of high-quality face-to-face discussions: seeking meaning, using evidence to support assertions, and building on one another's ideas. What aren't practiced are the skills associated with speaking, but "listening" is very much in play as students read the contributions from their classmates and take in the ideas being presented. When carefully structured and monitored, online threaded discussions can be an important tool for making meaning and promoting student interaction in your class.

What was your experience with online discussions during the COVID-19 pandemic? What insights for your own classroom instruction can you draw from that experience?

Questions Are at the Heart of Discussions

It's challenging to think up interesting questions that will engage students in discussions. One thing we know for sure is that high-quality discussions require both advanced preparation of questions and the ability to listen closely to student responses and develop questions in the moment to move a discussion along. It takes practice and can be unnerving for just about any teacher.

Questions can generally be divided into three categories:

- **Closed questions: those with right/wrong or defined answers.** These are used to check for basic understanding of the content and are not intended to generate discussion. They are often a starting point or are asked during a discussion to clarify a piece of information.

- **Open questions: those that are often called higher-order questions.** These sorts of questions don't have narrowly defined answers and instead ask students to interpret information, compare and contrast ideas, evaluate, synthesize, take and defend a position, and consider alternative viewpoints.

- **Process questions: those that are useful in moving a discussion forward or helping students to go a little deeper.** As discussions get going, sometimes it's best to ask questions like these that help students explain more or make connections with the ideas of fellow students.

  o What makes you say that?

  o Can you tell us a bit more about your thinking?

  o How does what you just said connect to what others (or a particular student) have been saying?

  o Where in the text do you find support for that idea?

Planning for Discussions

High-quality discussions are the product of thoughtful planning and preparation. This includes determining:

The readings, experiences, or other content that will be the foundation for the discussion
The advanced preparation students will be expected to do
The discussion format: entire class or small group? Partners? Jigsaw? Last Word? Rank order? Seminar? Some other?
What is your plan for an opening question?
Is it a question to check for understanding?
Will it send students in a particular direction in thinking about the discussion topic?
Will you have students answer sequentially using a go-around share with an initial thought before opening the discussion to the class as a whole?
Additional questions and prompts to move the discussion along

When you think about interesting discussions you've participated in, whether in or out of school, they most likely began with a question that had inherent interest or was framed to stimulate your thinking. That's true of the questions we want to craft in our classrooms for students to discuss. Good discussion questions require students to apply course content in the discussion and, at the same time, allow for multiple interpretations of that content. In the discussion students should be able to constructively challenge and probe the thinking and assertions of their fellow students as they explore course content more deeply.

This should be guided by your classroom agreements and expectations for how everyone treats and interacts with each other. Agreements provide safety and structure for engaging in shared inquiry. As discussions progress and follow-up questions are asked, either by the teacher or other students, new interpretations and understandings are revealed and subsequently examined. Reasoning and the use of evidence should take precedence over posturing and the making of pronouncements. Good discussions might become heated and contentious but should never devolve to name calling or intolerance because that's not part of the classroom climate you've worked so hard to create. If negative behaviors do become evident, stop and deal with the situation right then.

Good Discussions Have an Organic Quality to Them

Not all discussions need to open with closed questions that check for understanding and then move to open questions that ask for higher-order thinking. Sometimes a discussion can begin with a simple prompt to get students to begin thinking about the issues or ideas at play, such as:

- What did you find interesting in the reading/lecture/experiment/problem?

- What was confusing for you or puzzled you in the reading/lecture/experiment/problem?

- Can you pick an idea in the reading/lecture/experiment/problem for us to begin our discussion?

- Is the author right?

Discussions can and should be planned, but they also develop a life of their own. As this happens, facilitate the conversation by carefully listening to students and framing questions based on what they say. Listen to what they actually say instead of listening for your expected or desired responses. This allows you to think of new questions and build a discussion organically from student contributions. As you're listening, jot down ideas students are contributing so you don't have to remember all that is said. At the same time, you're working to manage student participation and everything else that goes on in a good discussion.

Plan time for the class to critique discussions when they are finished. One way to do that is to do a go-around share and ask each student to respond to this prompt: "During our discussion, one thing I noticed was . . ." Focus on things that students noticed rather than how they felt about the conversation. This helps the class take ownership for their discussion and improve their discussion skills. Take note of what students say and remind them of their observations and class agreements before the next discussion. If the discussion wasn't very successful, ask students to do the same go-around share, but this time to identify one thing they noticed that caused the discussion to go awry. Again, take notes and ask students what they might do differently the next time. Set those as goals before the next discussion.

Discussion Skills Develop with Time and Practice

Students don't enter school as skilled participants in discussions any more than they arrive with a full complement of literacy and numeracy skills. As with reading, writing, and math, students are less skilled in discussion at younger ages and improve after semesters and years of practice. There is a developmental arc in the growth of discussion skills from the very earliest grades through high school and beyond, just as there is from the beginning of the school year to the end.

Many teachers mistakenly believe that younger students are too immature to participate in classroom discussions where the goals are inquiry, meaning making, and greater understanding, so they shy away from making discussions part of their routine instruction. But younger students have ideas and want to share them with peers and their teacher, and many of the skills can be learned and practiced at developmentally appropriate levels in teacher-led discussions. As students see their contributions welcomed and encouraged, they develop more confidence and skill in expressing their ideas and learn to listen better.

There are many reasons why students of all ages might hesitate to participate in classroom discussions. Some are related to the lack of opportunities to practice discussion skills in actual classroom discussions, but far more have to do with social and emotional factors. Some students, often students of color and females, have felt silenced in classrooms that didn't value their voice or perspective. Some may have been bullied or intimidated by peers when sharing ideas that have been novel or unique. Students for whom English is not their home language may feel awkward speaking out loud or fear not knowing the right vocabulary. Commonly accepted ways of participating in classroom discussions might be unfamiliar or feel culturally inappropriate for some students. Most students don't want to risk being wrong, so they avoid sharing their voices or ideas. Negative peer responses can easily silence student voice. It can feel much safer to just remain silent during class discussions. Some students want others to do all the work. Helping all students to develop comfort in discussions is just one more step in the detoxing process we described in chapter 1.

Social media and the prevalence of cell phones with cameras also raise obstacles to student participation in discussions. Fears that one is being recorded or that something said in class might appear on another student's social media feed are real and can silence students. For some students, nonparticipation is the safest option. Here, again, relationships and the classroom culture you've built that values inclusion and safety to learn together are very important. Perhaps a new agreement might be "What's said in class, remains in class." Making sure that cell phones are put away for all discussions is also important.

We also worry about those students who might participate in discussions inappropriately by intimidating their peers or showing off to the teacher. Some students try to be the loudest voice to get attention or because they think the goal is to give the answer the teacher is looking for. Others do not have the filters to realize when they are droning on, or they do not know how to stop once they've started. These can be real challenges for teachers who want to bring student voice and discussions into their teaching.

Our job is to create environments where all these behaviors are addressed in supportive ways. Some students find writing, reading, or math more challenging. Similarly, some students find participating in discussion to be difficult. We don't forgo instruction in reading, writing, and math just because students are uncomfortable learning those subjects. The same is true for speaking and listening—some students are less comfortable inserting their voices into a conversation and some are too comfortable. Our instruction should deal with both ends of this spectrum. We need to help all students learn the skills of participating productively in discussions.

When all students are supported in discussions, we also help overcome the silencing and disenfranchisement of certain voices. This can be particularly important for students from racial or ethnic minorities, those who identify as LGBTQIA+, those in special education, English language learners, and those who are shy or reserved. Relationship plays a critical role because it helps you think about which kid is quiet for which reason and how to supportively bring their voice into discussions. Helping all students find their voice so they can participate in discussions is challenging. You want to respect individual choices of how to be in the classroom while also helping students develop these important life skills.

Here are ways to accomplish this balancing act:

- Have individual conversations with students who are reluctant to participate in discussions. Explore their feelings and past experiences with discussions and speaking in class. Listen with sensitivity about how hard this might be and then start making a plan. Suggest that they use some form of prewriting to organize their thoughts if you haven't set that up previously in a Think/Pair/Share or similar activity, and then give them support when they speak up in a discussion. Allow them to gradually increase their participation from only listening to saying something once during a discussion. When this is successful, acknowledge the accomplishment and slowly move the plan forward.

- If a student talks too much and dominates the discussion, ask why they need to participate so much. How else might they gain recognition in the classroom? Make a plan for how to participate more appropriately in the next discussion. Meet after class and discuss how the plan worked and next steps. Look back at chapter 2 to remind yourself how that conversation might play out. Suggest that students have a piece of paper with them during discussions and write down ideas so they don't have to speak each time they have the urge to say something.

- Start discussions with Think/Pair/Share or a Turn and Talk to help all students get their thoughts together and rehearse them with a partner before speaking in the large group. Then leverage peer relationships by having students invite those they just chatted with into the discussion.

- Collaborate with English language learners and special education teachers so students can practice for planned classroom discussions in resource room settings. You can also learn more about specific challenges students bring to participation in discussions.

Not every student should be expected to verbally participate in every discussion. On the other hand, every student should be expected to share their ideas at some time in classroom discussions. With support from the teacher and classmates, each student can find their unique voice. If students are reserved and speak less, that doesn't necessarily mean they aren't thinking. Some individuals find participating easy because they use talking as a way to process their thoughts. We need to respect both approaches. Never participating or always dominating discussions are where to draw the line because those behaviors are unhelpful in classrooms and in society.

Civic discourse requires all of us to contribute ideas but not dominate to the exclusion of others. As you and your students practice over time, classroom conversations and discussions become richer with the inclusion of more and different student voices.

> Describe your style of participation in discussions. How might this affect how you conduct discussions in your classroom?

The Teacher's Role in Managing Discussions

Behavior in discussions, whether in a small or a large group, needs to be constantly monitored, modeled, encouraged, and improved. As we outlined previously, you begin this process by spending the first weeks of the class helping students identify and practice appropriate small-group discussion behaviors. Integrate discussion into your lessons on a regular basis and shape student behaviors during them. More importantly, with each discussion, students learn to enjoy discussions as a way to participate in their own learning and experience working together as a class.

This sounds great, but sometimes discussions feel like they're falling apart, or students act out. When this happens:

- Stop the discussion and describe what you see and hear going on. Remind students of the classroom agreements.

- Ask students to identify the problems they see and offer possible solutions.

- Get agreement on any suggestions and a commitment to act on them. Proceed with the discussion as you keep monitoring student behavior.

You are using a conversation here to process what wasn't working in the discussion, just like you've used conversations to manage other student behaviors.

The worst thing you can do is announce in frustration that "we just won't have any more discussions because you can't behave properly during them." Giving in or giving up on discussion means relinquishing one of the most important pedagogical tools in your toolbox. With practice and structure, students can learn to be polite, avoid insults, and talk civilly with one another. Why expect anything different?

Control over the direction and substance of the discussion is a different issue. Despite your planning and your prepared questions, discussions don't always go as expected. Teachers often avoid discussions for this very reason because they fear that controversial or tangential topics will arise. You can't always know where the conversation will lead or what topics and questions might be generated in real time. That's to be expected, and it can be an asset. A student contribution that at first sounds off topic can be viewed as an opportunity to improve discussion skills. When this happens, pause the conversation and ask the student or students who have pushed the discussion away from the topic what connections they are seeing. If they are making connections that you or the other students aren't seeing, more power to them. What seemed tangential may actually be on topic. How cool that new connections have arisen through the discussion process.

If you see no connections to the topic at hand, it is your job to say so gently and steer the conversation back to the central ideas. Here again, relationship comes into play. You start with a presumption of innocence and assume that what appears to be a tangent might be a new insight or connection and that the students are thinking creatively. If the comments really are off topic or inappropriate, relationship helps you return the discussion to a more appropriate focus without getting angry. Try, "That's interesting Rosa, but for now, let's return to the question we've been discussing."

Assessing and Grading Participation in Discussions

Discussions present their own unique challenges for assessment and evaluation. Teachers wonder, Do I give a grade to students in large-group discussions? And if so, how? How do I grade students for discussions in small groups when I can't see everything they're doing? Will students take discussion seriously if they aren't graded? How do I give meaningful feedback to students?

Most discussions don't need to be graded. The discussion is the vehicle for students to learn what they think. The learning can be evaluated on a follow-up assignment that is the product of the discussion. Some teachers think that if a discussion isn't graded, students won't participate. With time and practice, students will look forward to participating whether they're going to be graded on it or not. They will regulate their behavior, deepen their thinking, and contribute to the class's success.

Here are some ways to assess student participation in large group discussions:

- Using a running log, note what students say during a discussion by jotting down the student's name and a couple of words about what they said. Make simple notes to capture student participation. You might note that a quiet student's body language indicated that they'd registered a comment made by a fellow student. One system is to use a check mark for participating appropriately. You can go back and look at this after class. Use a "check minus" for any inappropriate behaviors. A "check plus" can indicate some form of growth. Maybe a student who is working on holding back and listening more did a good job today. Maybe a quiet student who you've been working with made a contribution. You don't need to note something for every student every time. Distribute your attention to different students on different days. Give meaningful feedback from these notes, perhaps at the end of class or when students are working independently, to help students improve their discussion skills.

- Use student self-assessment forms. You can find versions of these online, or you can create your own. Many of these forms ask students to specifically identify and reflect on their behaviors during the discussion. Every now and again, reserve the last five to ten minutes of class after a discussion for students to complete the form as an exit ticket when they leave the class. Review these and, as appropriate, give your feedback on the self-assessments.

- When it comes time to do formal grades, create and distribute a short form to each student asking them to assign a grade for their class participation in discussions. List the criteria for successful participation. They should be expected to explain the grade they give themselves using these criteria and examples. Compare their suggestion with your notes and other observations.

You can use some of these same strategies for assessing and grading small-group participation. Wander the classroom while the groups are working and record brief observations. Give small groups short self-assessment forms. The work that small groups turn in can also be indicative of how effectively they worked together. Valuing student participation in large and small groups is an important way to value diversity in your classroom. In the same way that grades should never be totally dependent on student writing abilities, grades should not be based solely on student participation.

Tips for Improving Discussions

Large-Group Discussions

What if no one is talking? At first, waiting is a good strategy. Be patient and expect that a student will propose an idea. Time goes slowly when waiting. Let yourself be OK with the ticking of the clock! A colleague came up with the "rule of seven." Wait as long as possible, and then start counting to seven. Hopefully, a student will say something before you get to seven. Another approach is to wait ten to fifteen seconds (an eternity!). If no student has contributed by then, ask students to turn to their neighbor and talk about the question you've asked. Then ask one partner in each pair to tell the group what they talked about. Continue until students start volunteering to participate. Another option is to ask a question and then do a go-around, starting with one student and going one by one around the circle with the expectation that each student will share a quick idea or comment. From there, you can return to comments that students contributed to build a larger discussion.

What if a student dominates the conversation? Aside from what we already suggested, focus your efforts on what you know about this student. This behavior may be the student's particular challenge, and to meet or exceed expectations they need to include others, synthesize what others say, and use more inclusive discussion skills. Be assured that this problem will not go away immediately. Some students think by talking, and that's fine. It just can't get in the way of other students participating in the discussion. If the problem is going on and on, point this out to the student and suggest that they jot down the one or two key ideas they want to say to help limit their participation. Tell them to stop after they have said what they have written down.

What if a student never participates? Some students are satisfied with listening and are plugged into the conversation but feel no need to verbalize their ideas or thinking. In general, that's fine and is how many of us experience discussion situations. Sometimes cultural norms or language barriers might make participating in discussions more challenging. Whatever is going on, it's important to provide mandatory opportunities for every student to participate in discussions and small-group conversations. To ensure that a student has something to say, have them contribute after a paired conversation or a small-group discussion. Meet with them ahead of time and get a commitment to participate in the discussion. The goal isn't to embarrass the student or make them into a blabbermouth but rather to provide opportunities to verbalize thinking, increase the variety of ideas in the discussion, and develop greater comfort sharing ideas in social settings. Some individuals just need to be invited to share their ideas instead of being expected to voluntarily insert their voices. Provide that invitation!

What if students are all talking at the same time and not listening? First, be excited that students are engaged and want to participate! Then get the class quieted down and tell them to turn to a partner to talk about the question in pairs. After a couple of minutes, call the group back together and remind them of the classroom agreement that we respect one another. That means that only one person can talk at a time and listening is as important as talking. Hold these expectations as students start to engage in the discussion. If they aren't listening to each other, require that they briefly summarize what the previous speaker said before adding their own contribution. It's awkward, but it helps slow the pace and really emphasizes the importance of listening. You can facilitate this with energy and excitement—now you, then you, and then you! You don't want to do this always, just until listening improves and the discussions proceed at a more appropriate pace. We shy away from using objects that get passed around the room to signify who gets to talk. This intrudes on the flow of conversation, and when students are asked, for example, to toss a ball to the next speaker, it can become an opportunity for bullying or insensitivity.

It's always appropriate to stop the discussion and be clear that the classroom agreements of equitable participation are not being followed. Pause, let everyone be quiet for several moments, restate the agreement, and then start back up. You might need to do this several times before you see some impact. It might take several days or weeks. The good news is that the students want to be engaged. Work with that! You can also stop the activity and have students reread a disputed passage or write down their ideas on the topic. Then start the discussion again, basing it on the ideas they just wrote down.

What if a student uses inappropriate or intolerant language? Your initial response may be to feel indignant, but you can use this as a teachable moment. Keep a calm demeanor and take a breath. Gently stop the discussion and name the inappropriate behavior. State that the language or reference isn't appropriate in your classroom by referring to the classroom agreements and rules. A student might challenge this and say something like "What's wrong with that . . . it's true!" Here is a decision point, and a difficult one. It might be best to state that the offending language is not up for discussion. "We've agreed on rules about what is or isn't appropriate in our classroom. If you want to explore this in greater depth, we can talk outside of class, but my job is to ensure a safe and respectful learning environment for all of us." Another option is to decide that the issue of the language or the reference is worth exploring in greater depth. If so, table the planned lesson to explore what the student is saying, only if that is within the boundaries of your larger school community *and* the students are willing and able to do so respectfully.

MAKING SMALL-GROUP DISCUSSIONS MORE SUCCESSFUL

Make sure the physical arrangement of the small groups is conducive to productive work. This means arranging desks or chairs so they face each other and are close enough together that students can hear each other but keep the groups far enough apart to reduce cross-group misbehavior. In this initial phase, teach students how to appropriately move their own chairs into small groups. Give the group instructions before you have them move their desks to form small groups.

Be vigilant in walking among and listening to the groups. Scan the room for off-task behaviors, and challenge groups that say they're done if they still should have work to do. Listen to students without interrupting them and then, as appropriate, push the group to extend their thinking by asking additional questions. Help students know that they are fully accountable for their behaviors and thinking while in their small group.

Help make the conversation meaningful and engaging. Do this by providing a handout with questions for the group to explore or by assigning different questions/topics to each group and having them present their best thinking to the class. Use the following phrase before starting the groups off: "I've given you more to think about and discuss than you could possibly do in the time provided, so no group should say they are done until I call time!" Sometimes the work of the small group is narrower, perhaps to compare homework or quickly list ideas for a larger discussion, so assign an appropriate amount of time for task completion. It's always better for small groups to have a bit less time than too much, which can result in groups getting off task.

Require some specific task for small-group work. This might be a group report or online shared document they have to complete, a list of ideas they need to compile, or some other specific tasks. Collect these and include the completion of them in your grade book. Make sure the role of recorder is shifted among students. One easy approach is to have the person who most recently had a birthday be the recorder, or the person who woke up earliest or lives farthest away. When roles are being assigned, make sure whatever item you use to identify the person is an inclusive and equitable descriptor. A side note—this helps students learn about each other as well.

Begin with shorter amounts of time. Extend the time as students become more comfortable with small groups and you feel more confident in their ability to stay engaged with each other and with their task.

Use small groups on a regular basis. Reinforce and remind students of the expected behaviors each time. As with classroom management, expectations for small-group work need to be consistently and frequently modeled and practiced.

Post signs around the room with sentence stems that help students successfully participate. For example: "What I hear you saying is . . ." or "I agree with that point and would like to add my thoughts to it . . ." or "I hear what Danielle is saying, but I disagree because . . ." Refer to these sentence stems frequently so they become part of the classroom culture.

Trust that productive work is being done outside of your range of hearing. Small-group discussions shift the primary audience for students from the teacher to fellow classmates. When in small groups, students talk with each other and know that the teacher is valuing the skills of discourse and meaning making. This is where the student is being the worker. Students begin to own their learning and learn that meaning can come from interactions with peers. Plus, you want students to know you trust them to do what they are assigned to do.

Have the groups periodically self-assess and debrief about their work. An easy way to do this is a go-around after the discussion or small-group task to ask every student to respond to this prompt: What did you notice about our discussion/work today? Each student replies in turn while other students listen. Use this as an opportunity to have the entire class reflect on their growing skills in small-group discussion. You can also use a variety of self-assessments that ask about participant behaviors and individual contributions or even a simple exit ticket. You can find examples of self- and group-assessment inventories online.

Some Ways to Create Small Groups

Create random groups by counting off. For example, if you want groups of four, divide your class size by four and count off by the resulting number. If you have twenty-nine students, you'll count off by seven and end up with seven groups of four and one group of five. The small groups will have a random assortment of students. This can be more equitable because all students will work with a range of other students instead of forming cliques, which can lead to kids getting left out.

Form small groups in advance and read off names. This allows you to consciously distribute the students based on who does or doesn't work well together and to make sure each group has a distribution of skills.

Create long-term small groups and simply direct students to "gather in your assigned groups." Periodically change up the composition of these long-term groups.

Ask students ahead of time to write down one person they would like to be in a group with, and then have one of your group configurations facilitate that choice. For students who don't have a lot of connections with others in the class, give them top priority to be with someone they named to help them feel safe and connected.

Avoid having students form their own groups because students might be left out or feel less valued. Be intentional in the forming of groups—notice if any students are ostracized, if some students create cliques, or if you see a group rely on the same students to do the work.

What do you think are your strengths and challenges in using discussions in your instruction? What idea or insight from this section might help you?

Discussions Help Students Talk about Controversial Topics

Controversial topics take many forms in the classroom. A controversial topic might be the focus of a lesson. Or it might arise from authentic instruction without advanced planning because the topics we teach are connected to the world at large. A student might ask a question about a controversial issue related to current events or what the class is studying. In any case, you need to be ready to teach about controversy when controversial issues arise.

We advocate teaching about controversial topics intentionally instead of avoiding them or denying their existence. Most students are very interested in controversial topics, and these topics can find a natural and comfortable home in a classroom characterized by relationship, the valuing of diverse voices and perspectives, and persistent wrestling with ambiguity. Basic classroom agreements provide a structure for these conversations, and relationship helps ensure that the classroom remains a safe environment for all students and all ideas.

Teaching controversial topics and issues confidently is challenging. You not only need the skills to facilitate successful class discussions, but you must also allow for the rigorous exploration of diverse opinions. This is often described as allowing for a *best-case, fair hearing* of different viewpoints.

Teaching controversial topics can help students:

- Develop an open disposition to learning about controversy and practice skills related to civility, open-mindedness, putting oneself in another's shoes, and valuing careful examination of issues instead of relying on emotionally loaded responses

- Learn to navigate controversial topics in the society around them as they develop the skills needed to be informed and involved citizens

Our classrooms should be venues for respectful, engaged, and enthusiastic exploration of tough issues without the rancor that too often fills our airwaves and social media. The benefit is that research has shown that students who discuss controversial issues thoughtfully in classrooms have greater civic knowledge, skills, and dispositions and as adults are more civically engaged.

This is hard work, but avoiding controversial issues in the classroom can be even more fraught. As we began writing this book, a highly controversial Supreme Court confirmation hearing had just concluded. We read in the press that many civics classes studying the three branches of government avoided any mention of the controversy. What were students to think? Here was a significant historical event in the broader society directly related to the curriculum, but teachers planned no instruction in how to better understand it in the context of a civics course. We must take a deep breath, plan carefully, and engage with controversies from the past and present to effectively confront those in the future.

Do You Keep Your Opinions to Yourself?

What should you do with your own opinions and positions when teaching controversial issues? In chapter 1, we talked about maintaining certain boundaries between you and your students. Here, it is important that you carefully consider whether to share your personal positions on controversial topics with your students.

> I was teaching a unit on conflict and nuclear war to ninth graders. The culminating activity included learning about four different approaches to dealing with the existence and threat of nuclear weapons. The options spanned the political spectrum. Students first spent time in small and large groups to understand each option. They then had to decide which of the four approaches was most compelling to them as individuals. The final activity was to write a letter to the editor of our local paper advocating the position they had selected.
>
> Students pestered me about which option I favored. I had resolved not to share my own opinion on controversial issues, and I pushed back by saying that it was their job to figure out which option made the most sense to them. One class got to me, though. For some reason, I shared the option I supported and why I thought it was the best one for dealing with existing nuclear arsenals. Here's the problem: a

significant number of students chose my favored option when writing their letter to the editor, for the most part relying on my arguments. This was not the case in any of the other sections of the class.

Whether teachers should share their personal opinions with students is controversial in itself. Students want to know what their teachers think about a controversy. When teachers share their position on controversial issues, they can model how to think through these sorts of controversies and come out with a coherent and defensible position. In essence, it's a way of modeling critical thinking for our students in real time on real issues. If you do decide to share your opinions on these issues with your students, do so intentionally.

However, it is inappropriate and a violation of professional ethics to advocate on behalf of your own personal beliefs or positions on controversial issues. Remember, it is the students' job to be the inquirers in our classrooms. This is distinguished from a teacher carefully playing the devil's advocate or bringing unexplored arguments and positions into the lesson or even modeling how they came to their own position on a particular issue. As professionals, you'll have to make the decision whether and how to appropriately reveal your position to your students.

We take the stand that teachers should not share their opinions on controversial topics with their students. We believe that it's the students' job to wrestle with these issues in the classroom. We want all viewpoints to be respected for the power of the argument or the depth of insight rather than because it is the teacher's position. Keeping our opinions to ourselves, despite pressure from students to share them, also helped protect us from accusations of indoctrinating or trying to influence students. We believe the community expects that teachers will be referees in these sorts of discussions and not weigh in on policy positions.

Currently, partisanship and polarization are a challenge for democracy. Schools, as you know, often reflect the tensions and pressures in the wider community. People listen less to those with differing opinions inside and outside of school. One of the reasons we emphasize relationship and the building of a safe and inclusive learning community in our classrooms is to try and provide a space where students can differ with one another civilly and not with the rancor that has become so commonplace. When we respect and understand each other as unique individuals, we are more likely to listen to what each other has to say with honest curiosity and a desire to learn.

One of our goals when we began teaching was to "interrupt our students' dinner table conversations." We believed that if a student went home and at dinner said, "You know what we talked about in class today?" that this was exciting evidence that learning and thinking had taken place. We want our students to take the discussions of controversial issues home and ask their parents or guardians about their opinions. We want those parents and guardians to know that we provided a safe, nonpartisan environment for these challenging discussions. This transparency is one of the most effective defenses against claims that teachers are trying to influence students' opinions or are forcing their viewpoints on them.

Guidelines for Teaching Controversial Topics

Discussion is at the heart of good instruction about controversial topics because they lend themselves to deeper inquiry into the underlying issues. Just having students research a controversial issue and write a position paper is insufficient. Students must have ongoing opportunities to interact with each other as they wrestle with controversy and work to find their own best solutions. Questions of policy and how to achieve the best society are nearly always controversial. Discussion is how this process most productively unfolds.

Because of the often sensitive or politicized nature of controversial topics, you must take extra care to ensure that what you teach is age appropriate and meaningfully connected to the curriculum. If in doubt, ask a trusted administrator or colleague for advice and counsel. When planning and embarking on a lesson or unit that involves controversy, let your administrator know—not necessarily for permission but so they aren't surprised if a parent call comes in asking about the lesson. Explain your goals, outline the activities you are planning, and show how they connect to the standards you are teaching. Get the administrator's support and advice because they usually have a good understanding of the community. This helps them head off problems and shows that you have planned well and are prepared.

When a student introduces a controversial topic without your planning for it, what can you do? The first thing to consider is whether you have time to do anything of substance with the topic. If you do, begin asking for clarification. Ask students what they know about the topic. Try to bring in diverse perspectives. It's totally OK to tell the class that there just isn't enough time to pursue it further. Then make a choice to either build a lesson on the topic for the next day or simply move on. Honoring the student's question is important and doesn't need to throw you or the class into a tizzy.

Parents may challenge your decision to include controversy in your curriculum. Explain in your initial letter home or on the class website that when a controversial topic arises in your classroom, you will aim to provide a safe and balanced space for learning about it. If parents challenge you about a particular topic, explain why the topic is important and how it fits with the curriculum, standards, and skills you are teaching. Assure parents that you are neutral and are providing a place for students to learn about the diversity of opinions on the topic. Remind them that you encourage your students to ask parents or guardians for their opinions on these topics. If you have decided to share your position on controversial issues, reinforce that all viewpoints are valued in the classroom and you never expect students to defer to you or your opinion.

Not every controversy can be explored in our classrooms. Time and curriculum pressures limit what we can and cannot teach. Once you decide that it is appropriate to include the controversial issue in your lessons, the next step is to frame the issue as an open question for students to answer. You then need to ensure that there is credible information available for students to dig deeply into all sides of the controversy.

Here are some ways you can ensure that all viewpoints get a best-case, fair hearing:

- Begin by making sure that you are comfortable teaching the topic and have carefully planned a sequence of lessons to introduce and explore the issue.

- Identify and bring in resources that present diverse positions and perspectives.

- Play devil's advocate to make sure perspectives that haven't been raised or haven't been taken seriously are brought into the discussion and given credence.

- Help students see a broad variety of positions without signaling acceptance or rejection of any position.

- Take a brief time-out when things seem to be getting hot or contentious. You can say, "Let's all stop and quietly think for the next thirty seconds about something someone else said that made you think." Then have them share some of those points.

- Realize that some students like arguing for argument's sake and need to learn better listening and speaking skills. When this happens, require students to either restate what the previous student just said or identify something in the previous statements that makes sense to them before they proceed.

- Take time as a class to try on an unpopular position or one that students might not support but is held by some in the community. If the class strongly supports one side of an issue, ask them to seriously come up with and consider good reasons to hold a different position. This is the hard, but important, work of sincerely standing in the shoes of someone with a different viewpoint.

- Respond when students pester you for your opinion on the issue with "Regardless of what I believe, your opinion is the one that really matters here."

The reward for doing this hard work is watching students grapple constructively with tough issues and knowing they can do so throughout their lives. Imagine what it is like for students to have "aha" excitement and "I never thought of that" moments in these discussions.

Discussion: The Thread That Ties It All Together

You've seen in the previous chapters how classrooms based on relationships use conversation to help manage student behaviors, build community, and connect students with one another and with you. We've described how in multiple situations, taking the time to talk to individual students or with the class as a whole can help reinforce classroom agreements and build community. In essence, in these classrooms you and students are always doing a lot of talking with one another. And this supports the use of discussion as a consistent part of your pedagogy.

Regardless of the instructional strategy you decide to deploy for a particular lesson, discussion is likely to be a part of your planning. Engaged classrooms can't really exist without persistent opportunities for discussion! And engaged discussions are far more likely to happen when each student knows they are respected in the classroom community. This is why we say that discussion, and those many conversations with students and the class, are the threads that tie your instruction together. Best of all, it's fun to have meaningful conversations and discussions with students of any age.

Chapter 5

Assessment and Grading for Student Success

We teach so students will learn. For success, we assess to see what learning took place. Everything we do, including building relationships and being culturally responsive, should serve the academic, social, and emotional growth of our students. We use the information from various forms of assessment to give feedback to students and to inform our own instruction. Meaningful feedback from the teacher builds trust, structures success, and is appropriate to the goals and skills of each student. Assessment helps us do our job better and helps students learn more successfully.

What you'll find in this chapter:

- How to think about and deal with high-stakes testing

- Ideas for assessing in culturally responsive ways

- Ways that assessment feedback can improve student learning and instruction

- How to grade student work in more effective ways

- Why a revision policy enhances student learning and achievement

- Ideas about how homework can support learning while respecting the daily lives of our students

Thinking about High-Stakes Testing

The history of large-scale testing and assessment is one of culturally biased tasks and questions based on the knowledge and values that have privileged white culture in schools. This bias in tests has relegated students of color, English language learners (ELL), women, students with lower social economic status, and those from different cultures to lower status basic classes and limited future opportunities. Publishing low test scores in local newspapers has targeted many schools for public criticism and resulted in harmful and unfair comparisons between schools and students.

Mandated high-stakes tests take a toll on students and their teachers due to the pressure to perform well. Weeks can be spent in preparing for testing, with the results often tied to rankings of schools and even teacher pay and retention instead of authentic student learning. There are significant pedagogical implications in spending so much time and energy preparing for these tests. High-stakes testing regimes impact the emotional health of students and teachers and their views of themselves.

We can do better when dealing with required testing by leveraging our relationships with our students. Acknowledge the stresses students might be experiencing while encouraging them to do their best. Remind them that they still have authentic opportunities in your classroom assessments to show what they know and can do. Explain that because they've worked hard they bring a variety of intellectual assets with them when they take these required tests. Perhaps the best thing you can do in this situation is to provide the emotional support students need to approach this inauthentic situation with a combination of seriousness and self-confidence as learners.

Classroom Assessments and Cultural Responsiveness

All students should be given equitable ways to be evaluated and receive feedback in classrooms. Classroom assessments that are culturally responsive consider the diversity of students by remembering that language, culture, class, and gender influence what students bring to a given assessment task. Sensitivity about language and content allows for alternative ways to connect assessment to a student's background.

Assessment should provide students a variety of means to illustrate what they know and can do.

Here are several ways to make classroom assessments more inclusive.

- Avoid biased words, language, and references that privilege one way of being over another.

- Work with students to define learning goals that connect what they bring culturally and cognitively to the classroom. For example, a student who is a recent immigrant could bring their own experiences to an assessment in a geography class. An assessment for a neurodivergent student might allow for more time for the student to process the assignment or a different format to present what has been learned. This is hard but important so that you take individual characteristics into account as you ask students to show what they know and can do.

- Allow and encourage choice so students can help define and create assessments that will more authentically measure their growth and learning. Students have great ideas for what they want to do to show what they know. Together, you can then identify the standards and expectations for successfully meeting the assessment's goals.

Assessments can be more equitable when students bring their authentic selves to the tasks they must complete. For a final project one student may create a podcast, one may create a poster, one may write an essay, and one may do a speech. Checklists of agreed-upon criteria can ensure quality regardless of the format students choose to demonstrate their learning. Choice must also be balanced with our obligation to help students push through their individual learning challenges. When appropriate, developing writers need to be assessed on their writing skills and only writing will accomplish this. Even here, there can still be choice of subject matter, for example, as a way of connecting the student to the assessment.

Classroom assessments only have value when the teacher conferences on the feedback the assessment provides. That's how students grow and improve. When providing feedback and talking with students about the assessments they've completed, keep relationship in mind. What do you know about how different students listen to and respond to feedback? Be sensitive to how you write comments on assessments or talk about student challenges. There is a fine line between constructive feedback and hurtful criticism.

One of our jobs is to ensure that all our students know they are valued for who they are, instead of how they perform during state testing days or on individual classroom assessments. Our day-to-day assessments should improve student learning and authentically document what students know and can do, keeping in mind that an equitable and culturally responsive approach to assessment is mandatory.

Assessing Before, During, and at the End of Instruction

It's helpful to start a lesson or unit by checking in with students about what they already know or can do. It's easy: do a short poll where students select correct answers to questions about the upcoming topic. For a history unit on industrialism, show a picture of child laborers and have students discuss what is going on. Do a simple science experiment and listen to students talk about what they think is going on and what they see. In an elementary class studying home and family, ask students to help you list all the different types of buildings that serve as homes they know about. Because not all students are comfortable speaking, ask those who don't participate to write a brief note to share their ideas. These examples provide you feedback on what students know and can do in relation to a new topic and helps calibrate your objectives and planning.

Assessments are most useful when they provide feedback during instruction. Formative assessment, the assessments we do during instruction and over the course of lessons, gives us feedback that is used to inform further instruction. It is "for" learning. When we get feedback that students are confused, we can reteach or modify a lesson instead of pushing forward.

There are a variety of ways to get feedback for checking student understanding and improving instruction.

- Quizzes
- Entry and exit tickets

- Cell phone apps to survey student responses

- Self-assessment forms

- Thumbs up/thumbs down responses during instruction

- Written reflections

- Go-around shares

- Online surveys/questionnaires

- Individual conferences/check-ins with students

- Running observation notes

Formative assessments should never penalize students. They exist to help the teacher teach better and students learn more successfully. Self-assessment and teacher-led assessments should provide feedback to identify areas of strength, as well as areas for improvement. In classrooms where there are strong relationships the teacher and students are working toward the common goal of successful learning.

Formative assessment tasks do not always need to be graded. Check to make sure that students complete them, but assigning points or grades is not the primary purpose of these tasks. Instead, scan and interpret what is revealed by your formative assessments. Are some students consistently unclear about class material? Are you moving too fast for the group as a whole? Assessments provide feedback about these and other questions without you needing to assign points or a grade.

Summative assessments are assigned at the end of units of study to determine whether students can demonstrate mastery of content or skills. They are called assessments "of" learning because they show whether the intended learning has taken place. Summative assessments are things like final exams, final projects, papers, and portfolios. They build upon the feedback that has been accumulated by the various formative assessments during instruction. Summative assessments tell us and our students where they are in relation to mastery of course goals and objectives. Summative assessments readily lend themselves to student choice. Provide authentic opportunities for students to demonstrate that they have learned identified objectives and standards. How they show their learning can take a variety of forms and formats. Allow for choice as much as possible and be sensitive to your diverse student population.

In our US history classes students studied a sequence of events from the causes of WWI through its end with the Treaty of Versailles and then the rise of Nazism in Germany. The unit included interactive instructional activities and was very high interest. This unit examined how societies can manifest intolerance to those who are labeled and treated as different. The unit ended at the point when the Nazis began the Final Solution and the attempted genocide against European Jews, Catholics, Roma, LGBTQIA+ individuals, and others.

The unit's traditional assessment was an essay question that asked students to describe the cumulative events that lead to the rise of Nazism and the Final Solution. This assessment tended to privilege students who could write well. You might recall from chapter 3 that one student, on their own, decided to respond to the essay prompt with a poem that included the expected information.

To make the assessment support different ways students might show their knowledge, we created a recipe assessment that replaced a formal essay with a poster presentation. On other summative assessments, we required students to demonstrate their ability to write a clear and coherent essay. Choice involves a balance between allowing students to work within their comfort zones and pushing students to do the hard work to master other, important skills. The summative assessment allowed for individual student creativity.

Here's how the recipe works.

At the end of the unit, students were introduced to the concept of a recipe—that recipes have both a list of ingredients and a defined procedure to turn those ingredients into a final dish. Sample recipes were distributed to students. We talked about cooking shows they were familiar with or had watched. They learned that ingredients are in certain proportions to one another and that the procedures can vary from strong and forceful actions like crushing or mashing to very gentle ones like sifting or folding in ingredients. Students talked about ways of cooking and favorite dishes in their own homes.

Once there was a shared understanding of recipes, students were placed into groups of three and given the task to create a recipe for the rise of Nazism and the Final Solution. Students were allowed to use their notes from the unit. Using poster paper, they presented their recipes on the classroom wall. A checklist (see below) was provided so students knew and could reference the criteria upon which they would be evaluated.

Students had a two-hour block or two individual class periods to brainstorm information in small groups to meet the assessment criteria. During this time students reviewed notes to create a list of possible ingredients. They discussed among themselves the relative importance of different ingredients and, by extension, how to represent different amounts of them. They talked about how they would "cook" with the ingredients. What needed to go first, next, and later? Did they need to create procedures within procedures to accurately characterize the historical processes unfolding? Listening to discussions of course content in the small groups was an informal assessment of student understanding of the unit.

As homework, students then created their own personal recipes that demonstrated their synthesis of the unit content. When they arrived at class each student posted their poster paper recipe on the wall. There were a lot of them! The energy was exciting as everyone wandered the room looking at what classmates had created. After everyone had time to examine the work of their classmates, a whole-class discussion about common and unique elements of the recipes took place, which provided one last chance to review and discuss course content.

Grading the posters was much more enjoyable than reading repetitive essays. We used the checklist to determine each student's grade. You could also have a rating scale (1–5 from barely or didn't meet the criteria to exceeded the criteria) for each item and come up with a point system for the final grade.

Recipe Assessment Checklist

Ingredients listed are appropriate to the topic of the assigned recipe and include core content and/or concepts

Ingredients are historically accurate

Ingredient proportions demonstrate relative significance of each ingredient in creating the identified outcome of the recipe

Procedures accurately reflect chronological or sequential contributions of ingredients to the final outcome of the recipe

Procedure vocabulary reflects different ways that ingredients can be combined and processed

Procedure has logical coherence in the relationship of various steps

Mechanically accurate (spelling, etc.)

Some students are not as familiar with recipes but have experiences using instructions for assembling things. This assessment could be changed to create the instruction guide for assembling "the rise of Nazism and the Final Solution." Students would need to create a parts list and step-by-step assembly instructions. The concept of a recipe assessment can be adapted to almost any content area: a recipe for a successful music performance, for writing a short story, for developing a character in creative writing, for a successful experiment tied to a scientific concept, for solving a story problem, and more. It can work for intermediate students too.

Here, students received individual grades on their posters. Should there be group grades, and if so, how do you make sure a group grade fairly and accurately assesses all students?

Grading Is Different from Assessment

We said that you don't need to grade or assign points to many of the formative assessments you might use, but you still have to deal with piles of assignments. They could be anything from written assignments of various lengths to videos to art projects. New teachers struggle with how to do all that grading and all teachers dread spending their weekend on it. It's an essential part of our job, and there are ways we can take control and make the task less onerous and more instructionally worthwhile.

We think of grading as a bit like cleaning up after we host friends for a meal. We like sharing food and conversation with friends and we know we'll have to clean up afterward. In our case, facing a sink full of dishes would never stop us from the pleasure of cooking for friends or family and being together. In a similar way, fearing a stack of assignments to grade shouldn't stop us from assigning work that can help students make meaning of our course content.

Grading is the more mundane side of assessment. In essence, it is the assigning of points for work performed. When you teach with engaging, authentic activities, your grading doesn't have to be drudgery because you should be evaluating a more diverse mix of interesting projects. There are ways to make grading less burdensome:

- Decide that not everything students turn in needs to be assigned a formal grade.

- Limit busywork that requires grading as opposed to simply being checked in and checked off.

- Share checklists in advance so students know how to meet expectations on assignments and then use them when grading to provide substantive feedback and keep your comments focused.

- Assign work that is worthy of the time it takes to grade it.

- Just do it—get your grading done as soon as possible for your sake and, more importantly, because prompt feedback is tied to increased student learning.

One of the most important ways to maintain sanity around grading is to avoid having stacks of quizzes, tests, or writing assignments waiting to be graded. When simple assignments come in, deal with them as promptly as possible. Move them off your desk and provide timely feedback to students. Use time before or after school if you can. Take a moment before you assign something to decide whether it is worthy of student time and your time. Lots of work can be quickly checked off. If the assignment is a check for understanding, let students know this ahead of time and then give the work a quick look and put a check, check plus, check minus, or "didn't complete" in your grade book. In this case, the feedback that is most important is whether there is a pattern of not completing assignments or doing them poorly. It might be time for a short conversation to find out why.

If you are assigning work that is boring to grade, imagine how disheartening it is for the students to do the work in the first place. Assigning fifty vocabulary words is onerous and can feel punitive. Instead, assign five to seven important terms that will be used in a discussion or other classroom activity. Maybe assign different words to different students so each can be an expert when their term enters the lesson. It's unnecessary to go home in the evening with several class sets of the same fifty words to grade. A page-and-a-half to two-page essay forces students to focus their thinking and writing and is much easier to grade than a three-to-five-page essay. Ask yourself what is gained by having students write those extra pages. Assign longer papers judiciously and with explicit learning goals related to the extended length.

You preserve your time and mental energies when you give students assignments that are meaningful work. The work you require students to do should be challenging but not impossible. As we've said, when you provide choice in how to meet the assignment, students will be more engaged in their work and do it better. This also enables you to see more accurately what they have learned. And you get more variety in the assignments you grade.

Returning work quickly and using the school's learning management systems to track each student's progress provides opportunities to notice patterns of missed or incomplete assignments. If a student is falling behind, it's time for a conversation with them about how they're dealing with class work. *Listen* to hear why work isn't being completed and stay flexible in your response. It might relate to a situation at home that makes it difficult to do assignments. It might be that the student has organizational issues. Many students do assignments but can't find them in their backpacks or are unclear how to upload them to class websites. They may have technology issues at home. They may be using non-school hours to work to help support their family. Many older students have childcare responsibilities at home.

Because you are teaching from relationship, avoid making assumptions about why work is missing. Sometimes a student will say the assignment was stupid and they already know the information. That's interesting feedback for you. Ask them how they might demonstrate their knowledge and give them that opportunity. Maybe this will result in greater buy-in from the student. This is a time to demonstrate to the student that you are more interested in them as an individual learner than you are in their just completing an assignment.

Why You Shouldn't Offer Extra Credit

There are no sound reasons for extra credit. Teachers plan and implement courses of study with carefully determined pacing and substance. Work should be assigned with a sense of respect for student time and as a way for students to demonstrate their learning as a unit progresses. Work that is not completed on time quickly loses connection to the intended outcomes. Some students don't do the work as it is assigned and then come to the teacher asking for extra credit to rescue their grade. Extra credit reinforces the idea that the work you assigned in the first place was not really important. This is a situation where you should "Just say no!" What message are we sending if we say yes? Allowing students to turn in extra credit only reinforces poor choices. Students should learn to accept and grow from the consequences for not completing assignments.

There are other students who ask for extra credit who might already be getting good grades but want more work to get an even better grade. Instead of assigning more work, help the student improve the work they are already turning in. And if it is great, help them celebrate their accomplishment. There is no reason to give yourself more work to grade. Our teaching lives are sufficiently full without adding more grading.

When grading, feedback can build and support your relationships with students. If you expect quality work from students, it's fair for students to expect focused feedback that tells them what they need to do to improve the assignment. Students learn from descriptive feedback, not from a letter grade. The ways we treat student work and the comments we make on assignments are important ways of communicating respect. Slapping a grade on the top of the page doesn't support learning or growth. Avoid overwhelming students with too many comments and corrections. Be intentional and focus the feedback on what the student is trying to or needs to improve. Try to limit your feedback to a couple of comments on each page and a short final summary. Thoughtfully grading student work and valuing it as part of the learning process is an important part of our job.

Students can also help you focus your feedback on assignments. One way to do this, and to make your assessment more personalized, is to ask students what skills they want to improve on an assignment. This provides you an opportunity to tailor your feedback to the targeted skill and work directly with each student to grow and improve. A student has more investment in an assessment if they have some ownership in the process. A culturally competent teacher supports differences in the classroom by personalizing the assessment process to individual strengths and needs. One way of doing this is to ask each student to write a short statement at the beginning of the assignment describing what they would like feedback on. It might be writing that has more description, stronger arguments, attention grabbing introductions, more complex vocabulary, or solid organization. You can also, through conferences and other interactions, suggest areas for improvement. Your relationships with your students are strengthened when you are working together to improve the assignments students submit.

Checklists and rubrics help to make grading quicker because you don't have to write the same comment over and over. They help you provide feedback on what does or doesn't meet expectations. By sharing and discussing them with students when you give assignments, checklists and rubrics provide specific criteria to students for how to successfully do the assignment and later for what to improve. It should never be a secret what students will be evaluated on when they do an assignment. Checklists and rubrics make the grading more fair and less subjective by keeping our biases in check when evaluating student work. They help us avoid being harder on students we consider more annoying or more lenient with students we expect to be super competent.

Making Grading Fairer and More Consistent

Grading and evaluation are fraught with challenges for educators at every level. Take the grading of a two-page position paper. Your evaluation of a student's work can be influenced by your feelings about the student, the number of papers you've already graded that day, the topic and position they chose, and the quality of the student's previous work. If you gave that paper to another teacher to evaluate, the student would probably get a different grade. Research has shown great variation in grading between teachers. This doesn't mean that evaluating student work equitably is impossible.

There are a number of ways to help make grading more equitable:

- Make sure students understand your grading system. They can't succeed if they don't know what success looks like. Provide exemplars of work that meets or exceeds expectations and explore what makes them successful.

- Give students a courteous hearing if they think their grade is in error. They may be right! If your checklists are clear and your grading system is transparent, they will more likely understand if the grade was, in fact, correct.

- Do not give zero for missed work if you have a 100-point grading scheme. An F should be no less than 50 percent, and so should a missed assignment. It is mathematically unfair to do this. Overcoming those zeros is almost impossible. This is an equity issue.

- Do not have homework be a significant part of a student's final grade. A student might never turn in homework but still learn the course content. Most homework is either practicing a skill or preparing for a class activity. Homework can be copied, and there can be unequal access to parental help and resources at students' homes. We say more about this later in this chapter.

- Each student's assignment is a new effort, so expect the best. You might be pleasantly surprised.

- Have a policy for dealing with late work instead of making decisions on whether to accept it or not on the fly. Acknowledge that sometimes "stuff happens" in a student's life that gets in the way of completing work. Patterns of late or nonexistent work are reasons for a conversation, not necessarily a lower grade.

- Grades should reflect learning and mastery and not be used to punish or reward student effort or compliance. Students will say, "I really tried," and maybe they really did, but that doesn't mean they have fulfilled the expectations for an assignment or met identified standards. You can value their honest effort by having conversations with them about how to turn that effort into more productive and competent work.

Because assignments don't grade themselves, there is no "grading fairy," and piles of papers don't just disappear, create a system to do this important work as efficiently and promptly as possible. Don't let these demands sour your attitude toward teaching or your students.

Did the grades you received in school accurately reflect what you learned? What lessons about grading student work can you draw from your own experiences?

Have a Robust Revision Policy

One of the most effective and equitable ways to help students become more successful is to build in a revision process for assignments. Every teacher has experienced the frustration of the developing writer who keeps turning in the same poor writing, assignment after assignment. You've taken time to grade student work, put comments in the margins, and suggest helpful technical edits, all the while hoping your efforts will manifest themselves in a better paper the next time around. It rarely happens! Students aren't usually expected to do anything substantive with the comments we put on their papers. In fact, we spend a great deal of our lives grading papers, only to have students take a quick look at the grade and toss them in their backpacks or return them to online folders. Online gradebooks can exacerbate this problem. Grades on assignments might be posted before the actual work is returned to students. Students see the grade online and are done. To say this is frustrating is an understatement.

When you expect students to revise their work until it meets expectations, they have to take your feedback seriously. Without this explicit requirement, a developing writer just continues to produce poorly written papers. Likewise, how can an average writer get better if they don't have to wrestle with the skills and organization needed to improve?

The revision process requires students to do something with teacher feedback and comments. As they revise, they engage with your feedback to fix things as simple as consistent spelling errors (their vs. there vs. they're) or more substantive problems with reasoning or sentence structure. This is where practice can make better. You are providing support and scaffolding so students can learn how to meet class expectations.

It's also a concrete way to respond to a student who says "I tried" on an assignment. You're providing a chance to use that effort in service of an improved assignment. Just about any assignment can be revised.

You might be thinking, "Now I have to grade the same paper two or three times. Doesn't that add to my already excessive grading load?" We have a simple system to minimize that impact, and on balance it's worth a relatively small investment of extra time to get better, easier-to-grade papers in the future. It's also a way for you to provide feedback that students can actually act upon. The revision process begins with a clear expectation that students must revise unsatisfactory papers or assignments if they expect to earn full credit. Students who meet the expectations but want to raise their grade also have the opportunity to revise their work. Checklists and other tools can help students know the expectations for an assignment. The revision process comes into play only after a completed product is turned in.

The revision process has two elements. First, students must revise only what the teacher noted on the graded paper or assignment. You make clear that you won't identify any additional things to fix after the student submits the revised version. The student has to revise only what you said to revise, and that's it.

Second, students have to submit the original paper with each revision to get credit. The reason is simple: if a student is told to fix only the issues or section noted on the initial draft, you need to know what they improved. You can refer to the original for that. Instead of having to read and carefully review the entire revised document and guess what you're looking for, you can go directly to the relevant spots and note whether things were fixed or not. This dramatically reduces the time it takes to evaluate revised work. When work is submitted online in electronic form, the revision process can go even more smoothly. Students can more efficiently address comments, previous versions can be archived, and the teacher can monitor progress toward meeting assignment expectations.

A couple of other aspects of the revision process support student growth and success and make things easier for the teacher. To be eligible for the revision process and earn credit on an assignment, students must submit a credible first attempt. You don't want to encourage a slapdash first effort by a student who knows they can just revise their work later for credit. That is corrosive to the process and to your relationship with the student. It's also important to set a deadline for accepting revisions before the grade becomes permanent in your gradebook. This prevents the situation where a student ends up wanting to turn in all their revisions at the end of the term. In that case, any learning from the original assignment is probably compromised. Finally, set a reasonable limit on how many revisions of a piece of work you'll allow. Usually, three revisions either help the student meet expectations or it's time to move on to the next assignment.

The revision process is closely connected to relationship in the classroom. Teachers set expectations for quality work and hold them when students push back with "Why did I get this grade?" We know what makes for a competently completed assignment. Our goal is to help all students rise to meet those expectations, despite some students getting angry or frustrated at not being able to initially do so. It also addresses the issue of effort. Trying is fine, but you still need to work with the teacher's comments and feedback to create a final product that meets expectations. The effort can be directed to the process of revising the work with your assistance and that of other resources in the building.

The revision process can be differentiated for a broad range of students including ELL, neurodivergent learners, and special education students. They are working to show mastery of course content and demonstrate the skills expected in our classrooms. How the revision process plays out can be determined in conversation with the ELL and special education resource teachers, parents, and students themselves. You might allow more time for revisions so support teachers can help the student. Students might write initial thoughts in their home language and then work from there to complete an assignment. Expectations can be culturally responsive and attainable when teachers consider students as individuals.

The revision process provides a space where we can firmly hold our standards of quality while also giving students clear expectations and a structure for rising to those standards. The revision process gives feedback that says, "I know you can do better, and I'll provide the support for you to do so—but you have to step up and do the work to improve." This is a way to scaffold learning for all students as they build skills and eventually meet high, but attainable, standards.

> What do you see as the pros and cons of a revision process as we describe it? Do you think you'll use such a policy?

Homework with a Purpose

Homework should only be assigned when it has a direct connection to instructional activities or serves as independent practice. Assigning massive amounts of homework is not strongly correlated with student learning, and artificial intelligence (AI) platforms can make a mockery of most assignments. Although some parents consider the amount of homework assigned to be a measure of a teacher or school's rigor, it is more often disrespectful of the busy lives of students, especially teenagers, and unrealistic for most younger students.

There are some good reasons to assign homework. If you are having a Socratic seminar or other text-based discussion tomorrow, it makes sense to have students read the text as homework tonight. If you've introduced a new concept or process in math, assign a finite number of problems for practice so you can identify where students have misunderstandings or trouble. You can grade these with a check or check minus and this can serve as a great formative assessment. If you are flipping your classroom, the homework sets up the next day's instructional activity and gives the homework a definite purpose.

Engaging and authentic instructional activities inevitably involve doing work outside of class. For example, project-based learning requires students to create text, find illustrations, and combine a variety of smaller elements into a finished product. That work will involve doing homework, but it is homework in service of a greater end. A follow-up essay after a class discussion should allow students to continue their meaning making individually. The task has connection to the work that was done in class. When combined with choice, the assignment gives students greater investment in what they are producing. Many jobs in the real world require doing work outside of official work hours. Demonstrations of learning should have the same expectation.

Be conscious and aware of the impact that homework has on different students. A homework assignment that asks students to read an article for a discussion tomorrow can have inequitable outcomes because of the resources and skills the student has at home. A skilled reader might read the article in fifteen minutes. A reluctant reader could take an hour and still not have a sense of the reading. A student who is responsible for childcare duties might not be able to get to the assignment until late in the evening along with whatever other assignments they have.

Some projects could be very difficult to do for some students with no Internet or place to work at home. Culturally responsive teachers are intentional about assigning homework knowing it affects students' lives outside of school.

> What about our position on homework rings true for you? How do you think about homework?

Chapter 6

Relationship with Families, the Profession, and Yourself

Effective teachers shouldn't just close their door and take care of business within the walls of their classroom. An integral part of our job is to interact with parents, guardians, and families. Also, we connect with colleagues for professional support and collegiality. Relationships are as crucial for the well-being of teachers as they are for our students. The best of our colleagues diligently work to make their schools and communities stronger and take on the important work of improving the profession. To do all that we want to do in our job we also need to take care of ourselves. Staying centered and engaged is important for our health and our professional longevity.

What you'll find in this chapter:

- Why it's vital to develop and maintain relationships with colleagues in your building

- How to work with and build relationships with parents

- How to stay engaged in teaching as a career path

- What is the importance of professional development opportunities

- Why you should work with pre-service teachers

- How to avoid burnout and practice self-care

- How to maintain a healthy work-life balance

If you are a new teacher, your first obligation is to take care of yourself as you grow into the profession. This chapter offers suggestions for ways to eventually extend your activities outside the classroom. You'll have plenty of opportunities to do these things, but first you need to survive your beginning years in the classroom. Step up into these extra activities as time and energy allow, and step back when necessary. If you are a career teacher, many of these suggestions can keep you active and engaged over the length of your career.

Working with Other Adults in Your Building

We use the term *staff* when referring to the adults in the school, instead of distinguishing between administrators, faculty, and staff. Together, all the adults create the learning environment in school, and we believe *staff* is a more egalitarian and inclusive term. One way to be a professional and to build relationships is to be intentional about your interactions with the many other adults in the building. Each one plays an important role, and each can have positive or negative impacts on individual students and on your daily life as a teacher.

For example, think about the school's office staff. They have constant interactions with students who show up at their desks for a wide variety of reasons. They have a high degree of control over the flow of documents, such as forms for field trips or requisitions for course materials. They are in frequent contact with parents. These individuals are significant players in the culture of the school, just like the custodial staff and others who facilitate the daily operation of the school. Make sure you are respectful of the hard work they do and develop a working relationship with them to help make your job easier. They are a wealth of information and support. Having a good relationship with the rest of the staff is very important. Students experience the school, not just individual classrooms and teachers. Collaborating with other teachers and staff creates a more connected community. It certainly takes an entire staff to respectfully educate a student.

> In every school where we taught, we noticed that some kids spent the bulk of their free time hanging around with either the office staff or the custodians. For a wide range of reasons, they gravitated to these adults and developed great relationships with them. We often turned to these colleagues

when we had issues or concerns about a student. They could provide information or support because they had relationships with them.

We tried to be friendly with everyone in our building. There was nothing to be gained by ignoring people in our school lives or being intolerant of them. Life is too short to work in an unfriendly environment. At the most practical level, collegial relationships support the relationships you're building with your students. As you develop stronger connections with colleagues, you have greater access to diverse insights into your students. Another teacher might share observations about how they manage to work successfully with a student you find challenging. Many buildings have shared office spaces where you can consult informally with colleagues. Reaching out to other teachers and sharing what works with individual students is one more way of building the relationships that are necessary for successful teaching and learning.

What adults, if any, did you gravitate to when you were a student? What support did they provide and how might that influence your own relationships with students?

Team Teaching

One powerful way to build relationships with colleagues and improve your own teaching is to team teach. Both of us had several team-teaching partners, all of whom became good friends outside of the classroom. We team taught combinations of language arts and social studies, social studies and science, and social studies and art. Team teaching means shared planning and grading as well as shared daily teaching responsibilities. A team develops a rhythm to their teaching, and a new energy is created from the ideas and activities developed when planning together. This enthusiasm is brought into the classroom, where there are now two engaged adults overseeing the learning. You may encounter administrative hurdles to team teaching, such as finding a room large enough for two classes of students, scheduling conflicts, and finding a common time to plan, but it's worth it. In our schools, students advocated for more classes like this. Get your students behind you if you want to create this opportunity.

Not every adult in the building will get along well with every other adult. There will be turf battles, building politics, petty grievances, and outright hostility in pockets of the school. Sometimes you will have challenges with your team-teaching partner. Navigating these social tensions can be demoralizing. As you recognize these types of interactions, decide how much you want to engage in or avoid them. Sometimes you'll have no choice and will have to bite your tongue and go along to get along. Don't be a gossip and avoid stirring the pot in conflict situations. Other times, you can take a principled stand on something that strikes at your own core values. Most importantly, find allies with whom you can create community and share successes and frustrations. It's always easier and healthier to be with positive colleagues instead of joining in with the complainers. This helps inoculate you from some of the more corrosive interactions you'll inevitably encounter.

Some problems have to be addressed or else they get worse and harder to resolve. No one likes to address conflict, but if it's preventing you from doing your job or affecting your personal health, you need to confront the problem. A variety of approaches are available. You can ask the offending party how they would like to solve the problem and then offer some options, such as an intervention involving an administrator, counselor, or restorative justice process. If it is a bigger organizational issue and your administration is part of the problem, talk to a union representative or someone in the district's human resources department. See if you can form a school committee of like-minded people and come up with a proposal to move things forward. There is nothing worse than feeling like you have no power to address the problem. It's not helpful to just complain, so try to do something about it.

Administrators as Allies

We respected and admired most of the administrators we worked with. Administrators are crucial allies for teachers, and it is important to be intentional about building relationships with them. This is not kissing up; it's making sure the administrators understand and are kept up to date about what's going on in your classroom. If you're planning a lesson or activity that might spark controversy, let them know in advance so they can support you if a parent calls with concerns. Invite administrators into your classroom to learn about you and your pedagogy. Ask for their feedback on lessons. It's far easier and more productive to work proactively with administrators than to have to explain yourself after the fact. As a new teacher, ask your administrators about their careers and get to know them. Too often, teachers interact with administrators only when they need something or when they are being evaluated. Cultivate a good relationship if you can. They can be terrific allies. They have a hard job too.

Every school has committees that require staff participation. In fact, schools can't operate without staff involvement in some sort of committee structure. You have two basic choices: you can grouse and complain about the committee and the task, or you can roll up your sleeves and do what needs to be done in ways that respect your own time and that of your colleagues. One of the most toxic aspects of life as a teacher is being on committees with colleagues who either shirk shared obligations or make the work so unpleasant that you want to run from the room screaming. Be the sort of colleague and professional who takes on tasks and gets them done positively and efficiently. If you are positive and upbeat, it will influence others to be the same. Be the cheerleader for your committee. Committee work can be a way to connect with colleagues in different disciplines or who teach in other parts of the building. If you take the time to set up agreements for how to work together in the committee, it can be worth your while. End of sermon!

Working with Parents

Parents and families can be terrific supporters of teachers or cause us tremendous stress. During our careers, our interactions with parents changed as technology, testing, and a more competitive world influenced relationships between home and school. When we started, teachers seemed to be more respected and seen as experts by most parents and the community. If we had a conflict with a student, we were generally presumed in the right and the parents deferred to our judgment. At the end of our careers, this had flipped 180 degrees. It could be that decades of culture wars and the devaluing of education have left schools and teachers less respected and more vulnerable to outside criticism and parental pressure.

Parents appear ready to question the judgment and expertise of teachers. In a society where more and more parents fear that their children will have to compete for limited opportunities in the future, school becomes one more place to "fight for what's mine . . . or my child's!" When people's privilege is threatened, they have less concern for the common good. Regardless, a core obligation of teachers is to work as productively as possible with the parents or guardians of our students. Knowing students well and having positive relationships with them makes this much easier. Being positive, setting limits, and staying on top of each student's progress are essential. We need to assume that parents want the best for their child and that they will work with us to accomplish this shared goal. Culturally responsive teachers know how to interact with families in ways that respect each student's community and culture. We want parents to see us as valued partners in the education of their child.

Communicating clearly with parents and guardians is important to building constructive relationships with them. Collaboration with the adults in a young person's life is always better than confrontation. At the start of the year, mail or post on your class website your goals and expectations for the school year. This begins a relationship with the adults in a student's home. Be explicit in how they can communicate with you. Maybe you are OK with parents emailing at any time of the day or night. Maybe your school has rules about how and when parents can email or text teachers. It's important within any broader school guidelines to set your own boundaries that respect your need for privacy and time away from the job. As you set these and other boundaries, do so clearly, with a positive and collaborative tone. Life is always easier for teachers when parents are on our side!

Sometimes this takes a bit of extra effort, as John found out:

> It was my first semester of teaching, and midterm time rolled around. I was told that I needed to send notices in the mail to parents of any students of mine who were in danger of failing. I didn't yet understand the legal reasons for this,

and I thought it somewhat punitive, but I knew it was a requirement. To feel better about this, I decided to send out as many positive letters as ones explaining failing grades. I put them in generic envelopes instead of ones with the school return address on them so students wouldn't be able to pilfer them from the family mailbox. (These were the days before email and texting.) I sent a positive note to the family of a kid named Tom, complimenting him for working hard and earning a C, which was pretty good for him. He didn't much like school, but he was trying. A couple of days later, he stalked into the room and shouted, "Why'd you have to do that, Mr. Zola?" Taken aback, I said I thought I'd sent a good note home. He said I had, but his parents had never gotten a positive note from school and accused him of forging it! I called home to confirm that it was, indeed, a letter from me.

Let parents and guardians know about student successes and failures in a timely manner. Part of this is related to our earlier comments about catching kids being good, and part is a school expectation that parents be kept informed if their student is in danger of failing a class. It's also important to take time as often as possible to text, email, or call a parent to celebrate their child's accomplishments. It only takes a moment and is a powerful way to nurture relationship with parent and student alike. Using a classroom blog can help parents get to see what their children are learning each day. Apps and software options allow teachers to instantly report on a child's behavior to let parents know in real time what is happening throughout the day. There are options for chat boxes, instant messaging, and other forms of communication as well. Don't forget about the fact that not all families may have equal access to electronic communication. Be sure to stay aware of issues like student privacy and the aggregating of data that comes with some of these apps or programs.

When the news is not so positive or if the student is in danger of failing the class, communicate with respect for everyone involved. A simple formula is to mention a strength, then the problem or issue, and finish with another strength and a suggestion for moving forward. Be specific and have concrete examples so everyone is clear about what is going on. Convey that you are hopeful and encouraging when communicating bad news. The student is in danger of failing a class, not failing life. Tell the family about any available resources (working with you at lunchtime or after school, going to the school study center, getting help from volunteer tutors) to help turn the situation around and what specifically needs to be done during the remainder of the course. This is especially important as students get older and consequences can include not being eligible for graduation.

> Some parents or guardians have only received calls from school when their child misbehaves, breaks rules, or fails to accomplish some academic task. When they see the phone number of the school or teacher on caller ID, they brace themselves for the next piece of bad news. It's one reason a colleague of ours who has especially challenging students in fifth grade goes out of his way to make frequent, informal calls to parents to report on something good their kid has done. It might be turning in an assignment or working well in a small group or just not acting out during the day. He feels he's building a positive relationship with the parents or guardians so that when he has to call about a problem, they see him as an ally and as someone who also sees the good in their child. He finds these parents far more accepting of the difficult messages and more willing to work together to move things forward.

Electronic portals that allow parents access to teacher grade books and attendance records have created additional challenges for teachers. Parents now can helicopter over their child's grades on a computer screen and try to bulldoze away the child's responsibility for their own work. Parents in a panic can send excessive and sometimes insensitive messages to you. Here, again, is where boundaries around parent communication are very important. You need to be prepared for all sorts of queries from parents that arise from the information contained in your electronic grade book. Make sure it is up to date and accurate.

When interacting with parents:

- Take a moment to really hear the parent's concern. Sometimes what a parent intends as a question may come across as an accusation. Take a deep breath and respond to the issue, not the emotion, as clearly as possible.

- Remind parents of how to communicate with you as you described in your letter home or posted on your website at the start of the term.

- If you tell the parent you're going to do something to address their concern, be sure to do it. You can bet the parent will follow up.

- If the parent keeps pushing an issue, tell them you'd like to take a moment to review your records and that you'll call them back. Check your materials and plan what you want to say when you return the call or email.

- Let an administrator know when a parent is pushing the limits of appropriateness in their calls. The administrator's job is to support you in these interactions.

- Always work for concrete steps toward resolving the issue.

- Be polite and respectful, and never demean the student. This is their child.

As students get older, they need to take increasing responsibility for their success at school. Regularly talking with your students about their grades is part of the relationship building we are promoting throughout this book. When students are aware of their grades and your grade book is up to date, there is less need for parent intervention.

When parents and administrators are kept informed and as they get to know you as a fair and effective teacher, they will support you when you teach controversial issues or when you choose to look at content in depth. They will look forward to hearing about what students did in your class today, and they may even be a resource when you need help in the classroom. Cultivate your relationship with them.

What are your concerns about working with parents and families? What are some specific ideas you've gained in this section about working with parents?

Making the Best of
Parent-Teacher Conferences

Schools usually have a scheduled time each semester for parents to come to school and meet with teachers at parent-teacher conferences. Conferences provide another opportunity to expand your relationship with students by asking them what they want said to their parents or guardians. Kids know when they are doing well or falling short of expectations, and they can help develop plans before the conference. We would distribute a form for each student to complete, asking them to identify things they were doing successfully, where they weren't meeting expectations, what words they might use to describe their performance in class thus far, and anything they thought we might want to know about their parents to help make the conference successful. Student insight into their own performance is always interesting and helpful information.

Approach conferences with a positive attitude of building connection rather than dread. In fact, after conferences and meeting with parents, we often felt a bit more empathy for certain students who were doing pretty darn well given what we learned about their parents or guardians!

> At a staff meeting early in our career, a number of colleagues grumbled that "only the parents of the students who are doing well show up at conferences—never the parents who really need to be here!" In response, the principal reminded us that the students who are doing well were doing so, in large part, because of parent involvement. What a great opportunity to be able to celebrate a child's success with their parents. Yes, we want all parents to show up, and we make every effort possible to encourage that, but we should still take the time to celebrate successful relationships between home and school.

But this is not the complete story about parent or guardian involvement in conferences. As our own sense of cultural responsiveness grew, we realized that some parents who we would very much like to attend conferences do not do so for legitimate reasons.

Table 6.1. Challenges and solutions to parent-teacher conferences

Reasons some parents don't attend parent-teacher conferences	Possible solutions
Lack of childcare	• Provide on-site childcare. Student or parent volunteers can help out.
Inability to take time off work to attend at scheduled times	• Call these parents and make special arrangements to meet at times that work for them. Make sure childcare is available at these times, if needed, too. • Schedule conferences at various times of the day, not just after school or in the evenings. • Arrange a time for a phone or video conference conversation to accomplish the goals of the conference.
Lack of transportation to get to the school	• Conferences can be held at the student's home. • The school can provide for a ride-hailing or other transportation option.
Language or cultural barriers	• Provide translation services during the conference and for any paperwork related to the conference. • Invite an ally of the family to help with the conference.
Fear of Immigration and Customs Enforcement and immigration roundups	• Arrange a phone call or a meeting at a different time or place.

We need to be careful not to read into a parent's absence at conferences anything about their care or concern for their child or their commitment to their child's education. It perhaps goes without saying, yet we will say it anyway, that a productive relationship with your students helps you know why parents might or might not attend conferences.

There are cultural factors involved in whether and how parents engage with school at conferences or in other situations. Some cultures show respect for teachers and schools through active parental involvement in a student's school life, while other cultures show the same respect by stepping back and expecting teachers and the school to do right by their children. This is grounded in a trust that the teachers and the school are the professionals who know best what should happen academically for young people. To interfere or be too engaged might be seen as a sign of disrespect.

Another reason some parents or guardians don't show up for conferences is their own apprenticeship of observation. They don't trust schools. Their experiences may have been such that racism, unprofessional teachers, or repeatedly not being heard have shown them this is not a safe place. If they had negative experiences in school when they were young, returning to a school might be difficult or bring up painful memories. Parents also have a right to be uninvolved in their child's education. You can't force them to participate. As culturally responsive professionals who know our students well, we need appropriate understanding and sensitivity about why parents might not attend conferences or be more actively engaged in their child's education.

Be intentional when meeting with parents during conferences. Arrange the furniture to make yourself as approachable as possible. When a translator was needed, we always felt uncomfortable when the student or a sibling did the translating. In the first case, the student has a vested interest in how the communication takes place and may not convey accurately what is being said. In the second case, the student is put in an inappropriate position vis-à-vis their sibling. It also devalues the parent when you are directing your comments to their children instead of to them.

Be sure to share positive comments, perhaps in the classic "compliment sandwich" we described earlier of some good news, areas for improvement, and then additional positive comments. Have specific plans for how the student can improve if that is needed. Avoid education jargon, and slow down. Take time to ask if the parent has questions, and then listen. If the student is present, give them voice in sharing what is working or not working. Involve them in any plans you develop for future success. Be sure to thank everyone for showing up and supporting their child and you.

We walked into a parent-teacher conference with our son's kindergarten teacher. The first thing out of her mouth was, "Hi. I think of your son as 'the rebel without a clue.'"

We are still hurt and angry. Don't be that teacher.

Keep Learning as a Teacher

One way of being a professional and staying energized as a teacher is by taking advantage of ongoing learning opportunities that are available in a wide variety of venues. One of the best ways to do this is to join a national teacher organization such as the National Council for the Social Studies (NCSS), National Council of Teachers of English (NCTE), National Science Teachers Association (NSTA), National Council for the Teaching of Mathematics (NCTM), National Association of Multicultural Educators (NAME), or another professional organization.

Reasons to Join a Professional Organization

They publish monthly magazines with articles on content and pedagogy, including timely lesson plans and new scholarship in your content area.

They publish up-to-date curriculum and teacher support materials that are relevant to your content area.

They host an annual national convention where dozens of workshops are offered, from the theoretical to the highly practical.

State-level affiliates host state and regional conferences that are usually more convenient and less expensive to attend than national ones. Helping to plan and organize these conferences is exciting work, and they're always looking for enthusiastic volunteers. You might meet your future partner. We did!

They lobby at the local, state, and national levels on behalf of teachers and specific content areas. For example, the NSTA is a vocal advocate for science-based teaching about evolution.

Getting involved by networking and working with other engaged colleagues at any level is a great way to avoid burnout.

As young teachers, we attended our regional social studies conference annually and came away with new materials and instructional strategies. We also made connections with other colleagues that nurtured our professional curiosity and found networks of like-minded teachers. In time, we submitted proposals to conduct sessions at state and regional conferences to share our own instructional activities and ideas. We grew as professionals and expanded our teacher universe beyond our own classroom and building. We found that the conference sessions offered by practicing classroom teachers were usually the most applicable and useful because they emerged directly from their own experience.

> My (Jaye's) first teaching job was in the same junior high school I had attended. I knew many of the teachers, and most were well into their careers. They were very good teachers for the most part, but more traditional in their methods than I was. It was kind of lonely being the new, young staff member. Soon I began participating in the annual state social studies association. I made connections with some other younger teachers who wanted to teach like I did and who were sharing lessons and working to make their classrooms interactive and engaging. I learned instructional and classroom management strategies from them and eventually started sharing my activities at the conference.
>
> Later, I connected with a group of geography teachers who were writing curriculum with local university professors. I took Saturday classes with another university's International Relations department. They had developed supplemental curricula and lessons that were so creative and helpful. Because of these connections, I was hired to write curriculum on Japan and later to lead study tours there. These organizations taught me how to write lesson plans that facilitated better learning in my classes and allowed me to move beyond lectures and textbooks. They also gave me opportunities to share my professional life with other teachers. If I hadn't had those conferences and workshops in my life, I'm not sure I would have had such a long and enjoyable career as a teacher.

Most districts and regional education offices offer professional development programs. We aren't talking here about "prison in-services" where teacher attendance is mandated by building or district administrators. As with students, the absence of choice or agency only serves to diminish the likelihood of productive learning. We're referring to voluntary opportunities offered during summers and sometimes during the school year to improve your teaching knowledge and skills. Workshop topics cover the gamut, including working with special needs or gifted students, writer's workshops, Socratic seminars, using technology more effectively, and strategies for how to work with English language learners. Yes, this means giving up several days of summer vacation, but in addition to the learning and new skills, you can usually earn credit to move up the district salary schedule or earn credit toward state relicensure/recertification. Some of the best advice we got early in our careers was to work hard to maximize our location on the teacher salary schedule as quickly as possible. Those increased earnings can last a lifetime.

Consider offering your own workshop during the summer or on a district in-service day. You might have developed a solid lesson or unit that covers something in depth that would be great to share with other teachers. It's a little scary at first to teach your colleagues, but if you have something to share, do it. It's rewarding, you contribute to your school and district in a positive way, and you grow as a professional. Sometimes you even get paid.

Joining Your Local Union or Professional Association

Another way to stay engaged in the profession, contribute to its growth, and advocate for teachers is to join and participate in your local union or professional association. Dues are taken out of your paycheck, but it is money spent to support your own professional well-being. Unions and professional associations stand up for teachers and advocate for professional standards. In doing so, they are also advocating for our students. Advocating for good working conditions for teachers benefits both students and teachers.

Collective bargaining is crucial for improving teacher salaries and working conditions and protecting teacher rights. Recent history shows that as teacher union membership declines, teacher salaries, benefits, and rights are reduced. Unions and professional associations are there to ensure due process if a teacher faces disciplinary action or pressures from parents or guardians. They work at the district and state level to support political candidates who are friendly to education and value the work we do. Like joining other professional organizations, joining a union is a great way to connect and work with other enthusiastic colleagues. Teacher unions and professional associations are some of the most important voices for public education.

Unions and professional organizations are also important advocates for addressing gun violence and the horrors of school shootings. They lobby for meaningful gun reform and resist the pressures to turn schools and classrooms into armed fortresses.

Avoiding Burnout

An important part of being a professional is recognizing when you are becoming bored or burning out as a teacher. Teachers burn out for a variety of reasons. You get exhausted from the daily grind of planning, grading, teaching, and managing behavior. The inevitable hours of preparation in the evenings and over the weekend add up. Parents think they can email you 24/7 and expect an immediate response. We now are responsible for active shooter drills and fear for our own safety in the classroom. And the lack of support by underfunded school districts and anti-school legislation wears at our soul. There are frustrations with what one colleague of ours calls "administrivia"—the seemingly endless paperwork that flows across a teacher's desk or inbox. Boredom can set in from teaching the same thing day in and day out. Burnout happens when you are not supported by colleagues or the administration or you work in a toxic department or a dysfunctional school. These are realistic pressures on teachers.

The psychological burden of feeling responsible for the well-being of dozens or hundreds of young people, each of whom carries their history and challenges into the classroom, can be extremely stressful. Burnout is a real thing to take care of. If teaching isn't working for you anymore, think about how your attitude or boredom quickly becomes your students' boredom, and learning is compromised.

If you are unhappy or feeling burnout it means that you need to make some sort of foundational shift in what and how you do things in your professional life. For example:

- Change up lessons to avoid boredom and repetition. Jaye once taught US history backwards, from the present to the past. It was fascinating for her and her students.

- Try new instructional strategies to expand your repertoire of teaching activities. These might be strategies you've learned from taking professional development workshops.

- Take on different teaching assignments periodically, switch grade levels, or shift from AP to regular courses.

- Change schools within the district to get a whole new environment for teaching.

- Find and sign up for professional development opportunities to learn new strategies or learn more about social and emotional learning or mindfulness or cutting-edge educational technologies.

- Take care of your physical body and your mental health through exercise, eating right, and hanging around positive people. Get help from a mental health provider for support.

It might be that you actually don't want to be a teacher anymore and are just riding it out because you don't see other options. A colleague once confessed that he really didn't want to be a teacher but had just had his third child and bought a new car. He didn't see any option beyond continuing in the career that was paying the bills. To be trapped like that is difficult and deserving of some hard conversations with administrators and significant others to explore possible options. Being a student is challenging enough. They don't need to be instructed by teachers who don't really want to be there. We don't want to minimize the challenge of balancing the economic reality of needing a job that pays the bills with having to go to work each day not wanting to do what you are paid to do. If this is your situation, at least name what is going on and start making plans for moving out of the profession. Do it for the students! You might end up happier and more satisfied, too.

One of the best ways to stay energized and excited about teaching without leaving the classroom for an administrative or counseling position is to take on a different teaching assignment for the coming year. If you've taught history for a couple of years, teach a geography course. If you have taught intermediate grades, try primary grades. We have colleagues who changed entire content areas to stay excited about teaching. John was originally hired as a US history teacher but was interested in teaching more about world history. He agreed to teach an elective course that focused on Latin American history and culture. During the summer, he read and designed lessons for this new role. It was a great chance to learn, and a couple of his best strategies came out of that experience.

> A colleague at a junior high taught the same class to ninth graders six times a day and had done so for ten consecutive years. We thought he didn't want to have to deal with the challenges of teaching seventh and eighth graders or a different content area. His lessons were not particularly challenging for his students. As I chatted with the principal about my teaching assignment for the following year, I suggested that this teacher might take on a seventh-grade class for one or two periods so someone else (maybe me!) could teach the ninth graders. Word got back to him, and he confronted me in the hallway and threatened me if I messed with his teaching assignment.

Over our careers, we each shifted schools or other assignments several times. While risky and anxiety producing, these changes required us to look anew at our craft, shed some bad habits, and learn to integrate into new building cultures. John moved from a campus with about 2,600 students in eleventh and twelfth grades to a building with 900 students in seventh and eighth grades. The transition from older, close-to-graduation teenagers to the younger and far more squirrely middle schoolers was jarring, to say the least. There was so much to learn and attend to: shorter attention spans, a livelier group of students, different management issues. His next schools were a seventh-to-ninth-grade junior high school, then a tenth-to-twelfth-grade high school, and finally New Vista with ninth through twelfth grades. Jaye taught in four schools over her career. Adapting our pedagogy and classroom management kept us learning and growing.

We learned from these job changes that all students, regardless of their chronological or emotional age, want to have relationships with teachers and want authentic and engaging learning experiences. What worked for older kids could be adapted to a much younger grade level and vice versa. We realized we were flexible enough to learn new pedagogical landscapes and school cultures. It seemed, however, that the older the students, the more willing they were to just endure direct instruction and passively listen to their teachers. Older students know that the end is in sight and often have enough going on outside of school to put up with whatever is going on during the school day. Our catch phrase as we moved among grade levels was "The challenge of teaching high school students is turning them on, and the challenge of teaching middle school students is turning them off." We enjoyed the challenges.

As we changed grade levels, we learned that most strategies can be effective with both older and younger students. We had a high school department chair with an advanced degree who insisted on being addressed as "doctor." We heard she was mortified when we put in a requisition for boxes of crayons and colored markers to be used in poster projects in our high school social studies classroom. This seemed far too elementary for her pedagogical tastes, despite our students doing incredible art-based projects to demonstrate their learning. We found high school students initially reluctant to sit on the floor with poster paper and markers for an activity. But when they experienced how much more interesting it was to get up and move and have engaging problems to solve, they didn't consider it kid stuff for long. In the other direction, seemingly more sophisticated strategies like Socratic seminars and Scored Discussions worked incredibly well with elementary and middle school students who enthusiastically engaged in these serious and challenging activities that were usually reserved for high school students.

Another way we kept ourselves active and avoided burnout was by taking advantage of opportunities to temporarily leave the classroom for a year or two to take on special assignments like being a teacher coach or working in the curriculum division of the district. This is a great way to take a breather from the ongoing intensity of the classroom and from the daily demands of lesson planning and grading/evaluating student work.

John spent several years teaching part time and helping induct new teachers and two years as a clinical professor at our local university's school of education. Jaye spent one year as a teacher scholar learning and developing new humanities curriculum, a year co-directing a drug and alcohol prevention program, and half a year as a district teacher on special assignment in the district social studies office. We each had opportunities to serve as department head, which gave us an extra free period to do departmental tasks. Each change gave just enough of a break, change of scenery, or boost to keep us active and engaged in the classroom for our entire careers.

We also know many teachers who contentedly spent their entire careers in the classroom, working with students and engaging with colleagues. Teaching, for them, like for us, was a great profession!

Working with Future Teachers

One of the most important ways of supporting the profession and remaining energized is working with pre-service teachers. If you are fortunate enough to teach near a college or university with a teacher training program, this can be a rewarding experience. With the increased number of online teacher certification programs, even schools far from a college or university are needed as placements for pre-service teachers. From a perspective of enlightened self-interest, it makes sense to help train new teachers with the values and attitudes you value in your own teaching! More broadly, the only way that student teachers can authentically learn about the rigors and reality of teaching is by being in the classroom. Welcome these novices into yours!

Pre-service teacher education programs are frequently hosted at school sites. This allows future teachers to spend more time in the classroom watching actual students being instructed by real teachers. It gives novice teachers more opportunities for interactions with students and the chance to have those interactions critiqued by mentor teachers and university instructors. These programs are only successful, however, when enthusiastic and engaged classroom teachers welcome pre-service teachers into their rooms and make their practice open and available for observation and critique.

This might appear to be just one more burden for an already busy teacher, but there is a more positive way to look at working with practicum and student teachers. They bring an additional excited and motivated adult into your classroom to help work with your students. They shouldn't sit idly watching. Have them help with small groups or work with students who are struggling with a concept or a piece of writing and need a little extra one-on-one attention. They add another set of eyes and ears into your classroom, which allows you to think about your own pedagogy. When they ask why you did what you did in a particular instructional interaction, you get to reflect on your own practice. This helps you be more intentional about your own teaching as you model peer collaboration. Plus, we can learn a thing or two from these fresh-out-of-education-school newbies. They are reading and discussing the latest educational research, which might help us do a better job in our classroom.

Accepting a student teacher to work with you does take time and energy as they develop their instruction and classroom management skills. You need to set aside time for daily meetings to help them plan lessons, critique their teaching, and support their transition into the teaching profession. It's very much worth it!

> Did you have any student teachers when you were in school? If so, what do you remember from those experiences?

The supervising teacher often takes on the role of counselor or therapist as lessons bomb or classroom management falls apart. But this is how novices begin their journey to becoming competent in the classroom. If you are motivated by the ideas in this book, you want to be the person helping to develop your new colleague's pedagogy. It's in your own self-interest and that of our wider profession. An important caveat is that most teacher training programs require a classroom teacher to have three years of experience before working with a student teacher. We think this is wise. Get your own game together before working with a novice.

To help ensure that this will be a productive experience for everyone, take steps to create a positive working relationship with your student teacher:

- Make sure the student teacher candidate visits and spends time in your classroom before you commit to the arrangement. As they learn about you and see how you teach, you'll both get a sense of whether you are a good match for each other. Also talk to them about their educational philosophy and values to see if they align with yours. Conflicting approaches to teaching can lead to constant friction.

- Discuss specific expectations regarding daily responsibilities, attending faculty and other meetings, when they will teach on their own, and any other logistics.

- Establish norms for how you'll work together. For example, will you expect written lesson plans? How will you provide feedback on lessons? Will you team teach?

- Plan regular times to meet and discuss lesson planning, critique lessons, and troubleshoot classroom management issues.

Working with student teachers can provide a break in the nonstop action of being a full-time classroom teacher. Whether your student teacher solos for some portion of the semester or you team teach, most of the burdens of planning, teaching, and grading will be shifted to them.

Three Common Stages of Working with a Student Teacher

Stage 1: When the student teacher begins, introduce them to your classes and explain that they will gradually be taking on greater and greater responsibilities. You're building a relationship between this new person in the room and your students. Frame this in a positive and exciting way, and let students know that they are helping to teach a new teacher! During this phase, the student teacher is mostly an active observer and teaching only small portions of lessons. The activities and lessons are planned by you, and the student teacher is helping with grading and assessing student work. The student teacher should be developing their own relationships with your students.

Stage 2: The student teacher is taking on more responsibility for lesson planning and teaching portions of the lessons. They are more active in dealing with classroom management issues, but you are there to help, guide, and intervene as necessary. Grading and assessment are shared.

Stage 3: The student teacher is in charge of lesson planning, teaching, classroom management, and assessment. This is their solo teaching experience. Some days you are observing in the back of the room, taking notes to share when you conference together. Other days they are on their own in the classroom while you are available nearby. If you are team teaching, the student teacher takes the lead and is responsible for the bulk of the planning and assessment or grading.

While you are not free to completely disappear when your student teacher is soloing, this does mean fewer papers to grade or lessons to plan for a while. It allows you to sit off to the side and watch what is going on with a softer focus. While your student teacher is in charge of the lesson, you can pay attention to students who might be off task and gain insights into what's going on for them. You can watch classroom dynamics without having to be in charge of monitoring them. You can think about lesson ideas to suggest to your student teacher without the pressure of preparing for tomorrow . . . and tomorrow . . . and tomorrow.

Another benefit of working with pre-service teachers and teacher licensure programs is having opportunities to interact with program instructors, site coordinators, and student teacher supervisors. Without having to leave your classroom or building, you have access to up-to-date pedagogical research. You can invite these fellow professionals into your classroom to help with challenges you might be having with particular students or the class as a whole. Having an additional set of skilled eyes in the classroom watching your teaching is a terrific way to grow professionally and to open yourself up to collegial support.

> I (Jaye) had two cooperating teachers when I was a student teacher. One was hands-on, and the other left me almost completely on my own. Both were fine for me. The hands-on teacher brokered the change gracefully, though her students were resistant to losing her to a student teacher. She shared amazing lesson plans and activities and guided my classroom management. She was a highly respected teacher in the district, and I am ever grateful that she worked with me and other student teachers. My other teacher, who had been my most beloved history teacher, let me do my own thing. He had been such a great model in the first place that I had him in my back pocket all the time anyway. I loved closing the door and having those kids all on my own—a good example of a positive apprenticeship of observation. I had amazing social studies methods teachers who inspired and prepared me to start teaching with strategies that challenged students in authentic activities. I think classroom management was rarely a problem because I was keeping kids interested and actively engaged.

I (John) had a powerful student teaching experience in ninth-grade social studies. I can connect much of the success over my career to the strategies I learned from my cooperating teacher and the relationship I had with her. She trusted my instincts as she modeled how to work productively and positively with students. Back then, I had none of the language that we're using in this book, but I knew at some level that teaching was grounded in relationship and that instruction should be active and engaging. My cooperating teacher supported these ideas with concrete suggestions for activities and modeling how to develop relationships with students. The seeds that were planted that semester grew over the decades because she made the professional investment of her time and energy in me.

Only a very few of our student teachers didn't work out as well as we had hoped, and we were relieved when their time with us finally ended. In such cases, work closely with the university supervisor or site coordinator on specific plans for improvement. Provide the support the student teacher needs and, at the same time, do what needs to be done to maintain the instructional integrity of your classroom. This might involve stepping back in and co-teaching or having a discussion with the class about how to help the student teacher be successful. The relationships you have with your students can help you explain their responsibility to help this person learn how to be a teacher. Setting daily and weekly goals for the student teacher might also be helpful. On a couple of occasions, we helped counsel prospective teachers out of the profession when they were unsuccessful in their student teaching experience or found that they just didn't want to be teachers after all. This is better than allowing someone to set off on a career path for which they appear to be unsuited.

Working with student teachers can be a win-win situation and is one of the best ways to give back to the profession while also nurturing yourself. The energy and enthusiasm of these novice teachers can be infectious. They have a relentless optimism and curiosity about how to do this thing called teaching. You are there to support them as they experience the inevitable highs and lows of trying, succeeding, trying, failing, and trying again. We've had terrific student teachers, some of whom have grown into trusted colleagues and friends.

Maintaining a Healthy Work-Life Balance

The demands of teaching are enormous. This is evidenced by teacher burnout, low teacher retention rates, and high levels of stress. We are responsible for an unreasonably large number of young people who come to us with a vast array of needs, wants, and behaviors. We have to effectively plan, teach, and assess this broad range of students. We also have our own needs, wants, problems, and responsibilities. Just as we have to get to know our students to create a relationship, we also need to work on our relationship with ourselves so we can enter our classrooms feeling healthy and positive about the day ahead. Unless we take care of ourselves, we can't be fully available for our students.

A key to taking care of ourselves is being centered. We compare being centered to a potter throwing a pot. The potter expertly works to keep the clay in the center of the wheel, sometimes pulling up and sometimes pressing in. When the clay goes off center, the hands of the potter bring it back into equilibrium and balance. Being centered as teachers takes similar attention and effort. We enjoyed our professional lives because we set as a priority time for ourselves, which helped us maintain a balance with the expectations of our jobs as teachers.

> Early in my (Jaye's) career, the school district sponsored a program with the motto "Happy, healthy teachers make happy, healthy kids" that inspired and fueled me throughout the rest of my career. The program was jointly funded by the U.S. Department of Education and our state Department of Education. The district put on teacher health in-services and sponsored walks and runs on the weekends with a focus on improving overall teacher well-being. Teachers across the district would play together, meet new colleagues from different buildings, and invest time in themselves. There was also a school-based drug prevention component that trained teachers to organize school teams to develop caring and healthy school environments. The idea was that if a school environment was positive and safe and the teachers were healthy, kids would be less likely to experiment with drugs and alcohol. The training in drug and alcohol prevention and team building gave teachers skills to deal with conflict, stress, and self-defeating behaviors as well as to give positive attention to students. Each school

created action plans to improve their school climate so all kids could feel a sense of belonging.

This was a remarkable program. It came with funds for retreats and technical support and, perhaps most importantly, it had district buy-in. The program improved morale at Jaye's school. As a teacher, Jaye thrived on learning new skills, working on a positive team with others in her building, and eventually becoming a trainer for the state. This experience lasted almost a decade and was life changing for her and many others.

Teaching can be isolating, so working on a team with a unified vision was extremely supportive and helped to limit teacher negativity that can so easily thrive in schools. It saddened Jaye to see colleagues who were never excited about solving problems, never helped to better their school, and felt they knew it all. The dismissive comment "We've tried this before" was depressing to hear. Had these teachers given up on change? Were they no longer interested in improving their school and themselves?

When you're positive, healthy, and take care of yourself, you can bring your whole self to the classroom. It's easy to feel stress as a teacher and have a sense of not being able to do it all. We are *on* every day, all day, with limited time to prepare lessons and grade work as we try to maintain lives of our own. Part of the centering process is honestly addressing these aspects of our life and figuring out ways to stay healthy. We have to practice self-care by allowing ourselves to be more important than our never-ending to-do lists. There is always more to do, and it can feel like so much of our professional life is out of our control. Creating and working on a balance between our job and our out-of-school life takes attention and persistence.

Exercise is one way to help take care of your emotional and psychological self. This is a challenge because there is so little time in a teacher's day to eat right and exercise. We were better teachers because we made exercise a priority. It helped us be healthier, more present, and more centered as teachers.

The period right after lunch was the toughest—and those three to five o'clock slumps with heads nodding during faculty meetings. A commitment to exercise helped Jaye find the energy she needed all day, and especially for the end of the day:

Remember those district-sponsored runs? I met a colleague on a school sponsored run who agreed to run with me in the mornings before school. We did it four days a week at 5:00 a.m. if the temperature was above twenty degrees and there was no snow. I'd set my alarm for 4:45, throw on my clothes, and drive the seven minutes to her house. We'd run for an hour, and I'd be home by 6:10. The next morning, she would meet me at my house at 5:00. This gave me a few more minutes of sleep before we ran. In the twenty-five years of doing this, we each overslept only once. No one needed us until 6:30, and it was my time for myself. It energized me during the day and gave me mental tranquility. Not only did I have someone to talk to about school, relationships, and life, but I also exercised my dog! This was a pretty significant commitment, but it worked for me.

Physical exercise is certainly one way to stay mentally and physically healthy. Figure out how you can do something within your abilities that supports positive mental health efforts—a friend, a class, an app. Put yourself at the top of your to-do list at some point in your day. It doesn't need to be so early in the morning. It doesn't need to be a marathon. Walk at lunch with a colleague, sit outside in fresh air for your planning period, ride a bike to school, reserve time each day for reading for pleasure, or sign up for an early evening class at a gym or yoga studio.

Packing our lunch every day was one way we made sure we got our fruits and vegetables. We can't tell you how many times we hurried down the hall to a lunch meeting balancing a sandwich, carrot sticks, and an apple. When we were teachers, school lunches were not known to be healthy, so we avoided them (except on days when they served chili and a cinnamon roll!) and tried not to snack at our desks. We're excited that school lunches in some places are becoming healthier, but we liked feeling that we were nourishing ourselves. On the other hand, not having to worry about packing a lunch might be an easy way to take a responsibility literally off your plate in the morning. Figure out what works for you.

A crucial part of staying centered is being okay with saying no. Earlier in this chapter, we talked about the importance of stepping up and taking on committee work or participating in other professional activities. This is a balancing game. You shouldn't hole up in your room and never contribute to your community, but you also have to say no at times to avoid getting stretched too thin. If you are like the teacher we describe in this book, everyone will want you to be on their committee. We loved being involved in our schools. We liked committee work and supervised clubs for students, but sometimes you have to set a limit and say no. It's also easier to say no if you've already said yes on a number of occasions.

Self-care involves paying attention to your mental health and well-being. As teachers, our switches tend to always be on and stress is just part of our daily existence. You can support yourself through mindfulness or meditation practice. It's a way to calm yourself, find your center, reduce stress, and build a greater capacity to be present throughout the day. There are apps, classes, and courses that can help you learn how to do this.

Developing a practice can ground you and stabilize you in a world that pulls at you for your attention every minute. This quote from Maya Angelou is a great way to start your day: "This is a beautiful day. I've never seen it before." It's too easy to wake up every morning and think "Here I go again." If you believe every day is a new today, it's easier to be in the moment. Instead of "I have to get through this lesson," think about what will be new this time. It feels much better to free yourself from negativity or being overly critical and frustrated. Starting each day as a new, unknown, potentially good day goes a long way in helping your mental health and well-being.

> What are your challenges in staying centered and healthy now? What can you do about that?

Setting Realistic Goals for Yourself

There are two kinds of satisfaction. One is based on results and the other on process. With a results focus, we feel good when we achieve a certain goal and accomplish the desired end product. A downside is that those who focus on outcomes may experience failure more deeply, be dissatisfied with the result, or even look for reasons to blame others for the lack of results. When we finish a unit but the students didn't do well on the test, we tend to blame someone—ourselves or the students. After trying a new activity and having it bomb, it's easy to resort to the tried and true in hopes of getting better results.

We found that our job was easier when we focused on the process of teaching instead of only measuring success by the end results. It was more satisfying for us to be involved in the moment-by-moment process of teaching instead of always worrying about the next assessment. We were able to focus our energy and attention more on what students were actually saying and doing, which is critical to supporting them as they engaged in our classrooms. When you're not solely focused on how things will turn out, you can deal with a lesson that failed by learning from it and trying it again another day. Let the process of teaching moment by moment be satisfying. That is one way to experience the joy and humor in what we do. It allows time to have fun with students, pursue digressions, and then get back into the lesson. It's having a teaching life by living a centered life.

It is so easy to be overly critical of yourself as a teacher. We can't be perfectionists if we want to be healthy teachers. Teachers continually say to themselves, "If only I could do more, do better, do one more thing to connect with that one kid." We tried to reach every student, but sometimes you just have to admit that you might not be the person a particular kid is going to connect with in that time and space. It's hard to admit but important to do at some point. It's another way of being centered. The good news is that there are many other adults in the building with whom that kid might connect.

We have seen teachers take on too much responsibility for a student's success to the point of enabling and disempowering them. This isn't healthy. Going back to our discussion on boundaries, you need to be aware of when you are taking on a student's problems. Instead, find resources in the building to support their social and emotional needs. Sometimes issues are larger than we can handle as classroom teachers. An important part of being centered as a teacher is recognizing the limited role you can play in a student's life.

Another way to remain centered is to avoid the stamp collecting we talked about in chapter 2. If you believe that every day is a new day, then the kid who was testing you yesterday can walk into class today and be greeted with a smile. As teachers who value relationship, it's our responsibility to keep that relationship alive and hope for a positive change in behavior. You can be more positive if you don't collect the negative and frustrating events of the workday and carry them with you day after day. The abrasive student, the lazy staff member, the rigid administrator can all get a new chance to succeed with you. You have much more control over your life as a classroom teacher when you know that regardless of the negativity of those around you, you have the attitude that everyone deserves the right to try and do better the next time. Giving in to negativity throws you off center.

Don't focus solely on being the best teacher possible. Try to the best *person* possible. If you enter your classroom with positive self-talk, you are in the game. Be kind, be nice, be approachable, have fun, listen. Laugh, smile, and show your delight in these wonderful humans occupying the space in your room. As we highlighted in chapter 1, make time to learn who your students are by listening to and engaging with them. Let them know you want to like them. Get to know them outside the classroom—in clubs, intramurals, or school projects. Make your classroom a great place to be for you and your students. Who wants to go to work where there is no connection, no joy, or no chance to be who you really are?

At the end of the day, being centered helps you find the unlimited joy in teaching and building relationships. To bring your whole person to the classroom, you need to take care of yourself. Find ways to be healthy mentally and physically. Be kind to yourself and make time to play, learn something new, and connect with positive colleagues. Check to see if your students are doing more work than you in your classroom. Remember that the student is the worker. Having balance in your life provides the opportunity for every day to be a new, beautiful today.

Final Words of Encouragement

We started this book declaring that teaching is a great profession. It is, but it's not easy or stress-free. When teaching is based in relationships with students, colleagues, and families, we work in a world of worthwhile human connection. We are agents of change and stewards of our democratic traditions. We teach skills that are valuable throughout a person's life and help promote a civil society. We value engaged and disengaged students alike, and we honor the diverse ways of being that our students from all backgrounds bring into our classroom and our life. The work we do to be culturally responsive, democracy supporting teachers inspires us to do better. We create engaging learning activities and foster discussions to help young people become better thinkers who can share their thoughts and insights with clarity and confidence. We take care of ourselves so we can be the best person we can be. Teachers do incredibly important work nurturing children who are our most important national resource. You can do this! *Teaching is a great profession.*

Acknowledgments

From Both of Us

This book is a product of all the collective work we and others have done to make teaching a great profession. Thank you to our students and fellow staff members at the many schools where we've taught. We had a lifetime of enjoyment working with and learning from you. We have many to thank. To John Thompson, principal at Base Line Junior High School, who allowed us to job share, thus beginning our professional collaboration, and to Dick Werpy, our first job sharing principal, for his friendship and guidance. To our colleagues at the University of Colorado School of Education who gave us the opportunity to teach methods classes and sharpen our own skills in working with prospective teachers. This book probably would not exist were it not for the opportunity to help create and teach at New Vista High School. We fondly remember Dean Damon, the superintendent who launched the school, for his vision, compassion, and friendship. To our colleagues at New Vista—our sincerest appreciation for your dedication to your craft, to the students over the years, and to the vision of the school. To high school teachers Andy Aiken and Bob LaRue, valued colleagues, for the deeply engaging activities they developed in more traditional teaching environments. And to our friends both in and out of education with whom we talked about teaching on runs, bike rides, and around the dinner table.

We so appreciate the many readers who provided feedback on the early drafts of the book: Mark Baildon, Anna Blanco, Deann Bucher, Anissa Butler, Mariana Castro, David Chrislip, Tom Gilboy, Lynn Glueck, Diana Hess, Tim Hillmer, Christina Trager, Amanda Metcalf, Barbara Miller, Rona Wilensky, Carol Wilson, and Peter Zola. This book is better because of the investment of your time, knowledge, and collegiality. We are profoundly grateful to the amazing Ina Chang, who supported and assisted us in crafting this book, and Rica Asuncion-Reed for her assistance with the manuscript. Thank you to Kevin Welner for connecting us to Richard Carlin at SUNY Press. No list of appreciations can ever be totally complete. To those we mistakenly omitted, our apologies.

Jaye

I always wanted to be a teacher. My second-grade teacher, Ms. Baurenschmidt, and my sixth-grade teacher, Ms. Hewitt, were teachers who made me love learning and I loved them. My junior high teachers (too many to name) inspired me. Like the hard teacher described in this book, they helped me grow, learn, and gain confidence in myself. But truly the model for the teacher I am today is my high school social studies teacher, Tom Shaw. His wit, his breadth of curiosity, and his probing questions inspired and challenged me. A friend forever, I am influenced by him daily. He became my cooperating teacher along with Paula Prentup and together they modeled and nurtured the important skills of being a teacher. My college methods instructors coached me to create authentic, engaging lessons. I think Jack Cousins, Matt Downey, John Haas, and Dick Kraft would appreciate this book and my career. I hold dear my team-teaching colleagues who made teaching an adventure every day: Dorothy Scornavacco, Anissa Butler, Joel Simon, and Marco de Martino. Teaching with my many colleagues at New Vista pushed me and helped me to put into practice the ideas in this book. I am honored to have been a part of that teaching community. I want to thank Jim and Sharryl Davis at the Social Science Educational Consortium, the USDE School Team Approach trainers, Lynn Parisi at the Program for Teaching East Asia, and Marianne Kenny at the Colorado Department of Education and others who gave me the opportunities to write curriculum and/or teach teachers. This book represents your support and the opportunities you gave me. Thank you.

John

Thank you to Fred Newman, Gary Wehlage, Alan Lockwood, and David Harris at the University of Wisconsin where I first learned to be a teacher. On a lark, John Pare introduced me to my cooperating teacher, Marsha Stewart. Working with Marsha defined my career and showed me I could become the teacher I wanted to be. Ranne Dwyer, Tom Tonnesen, Nancy Vojtik, and Bob Laabs, my first colleagues at Waukesha South High School, were kind and generous to a very young and inexperienced rookie teacher. A special thanks to Bruce Scotland, my nearest and dearest colleague, friend, and roommate. I can't imagine any better person with whom to begin my journey as a teacher and to have along for the entire ride. Mike Hartoonian encouraged and supported my journey to Boulder to become a teacher associate at the Social Science Education Consortium. Thanks to Doug Superka, Sharryl Hawke-Davis, Jim Davis, Bruce Tipple, Ron Schukar, and others from my days at the Social Science Education Consortium and Center for Teaching International Relations. You expanded my skills and my horizons as a teacher, curriculum developer, and workshop presenter and became lifelong friends. To the social studies department at Campus Middle Unit, where I learned the joys and challenges of teaching seventh and eighth graders. In particular, to Jackie Johnson, who advocated for me to be hired there. Rona Wilensky brought Socratic seminars into my teaching practice and was our valued principal at New Vista. Thanks to Andrew Pfouts for being a tremendous team-teaching partner. It was in the community of New Vista where the ideas in this book came to full fruition. It was fun and good work to be a part of the staff.

Index

215